Jonathan Jones
Murray–Darling views

Surpllus

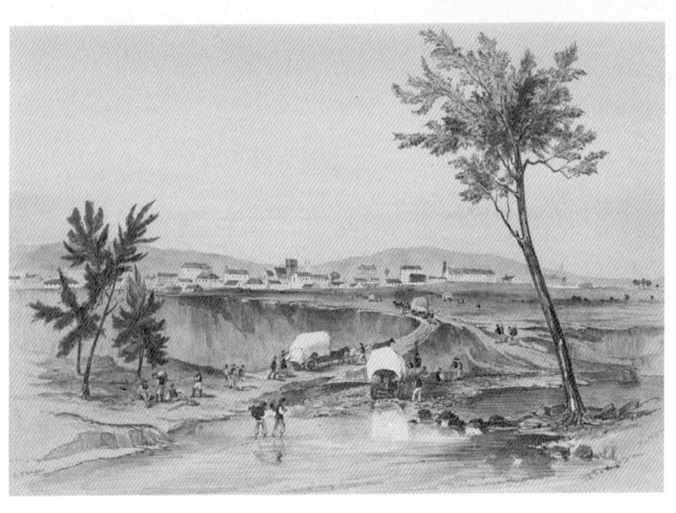

GEORGE FRENCH ANGAS
England / Australia
born Newcastle-upon-Tyne, England, 1822
died London, England, 1886
Bathurst c. 1868
Wiradjuri country, Bathurst, New South Wales
hand-coloured lithograph on paper
22.9 × 33.9 cm
David Murray Bequest Fund 1964
Art Gallery of South Australia, Adelaide
646G22

MAKING A CANOE

Many people who had never seen a canoe made by the Murray River natives had the idea that its construction was a simple process;

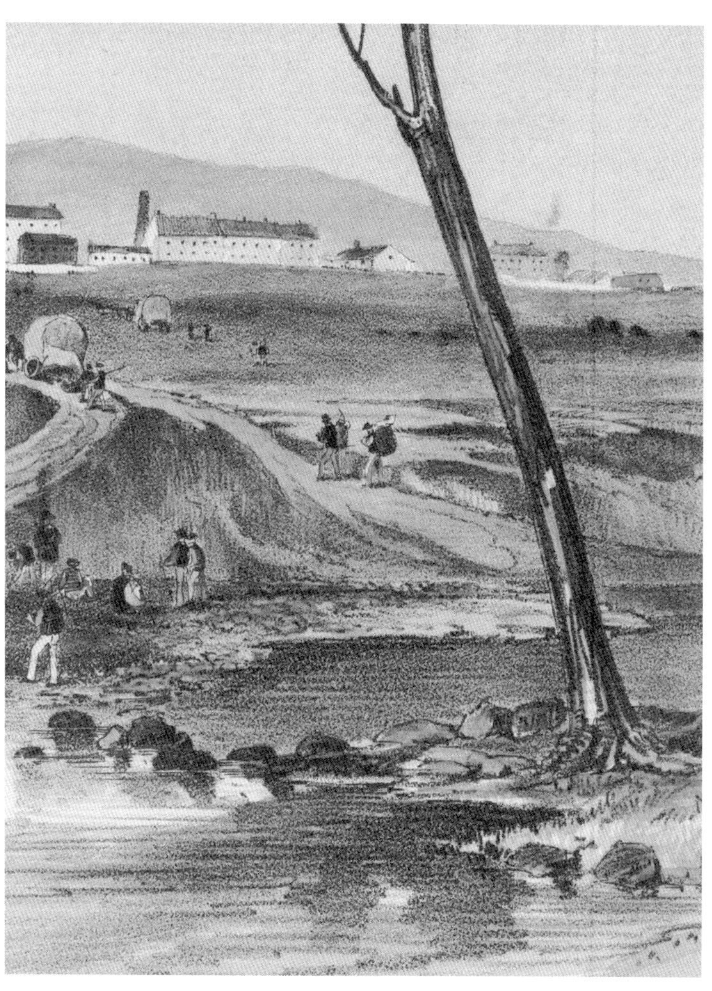

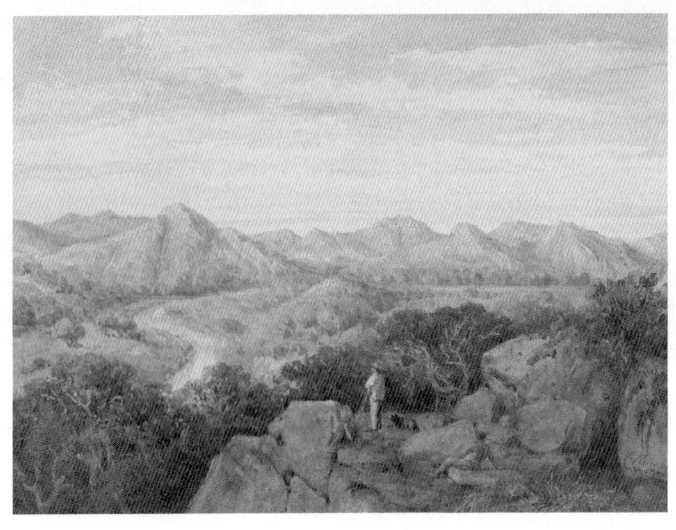

LOUIS BUVELOT
Switzerland / Australia / Brazil
born Morges, Switzerland, 1814
died Melbourne, Australia, 1888
Murrumbidgee River 1870s
Wiradjuri country, New South Wales
watercolour on paper
24.8 × 35 cm
M.J.M. Carter AO Collection 2004
Art Gallery of South Australia, Adelaide
20044P14

but, on the contrary, a good deal of judgment was required in the manufacture.

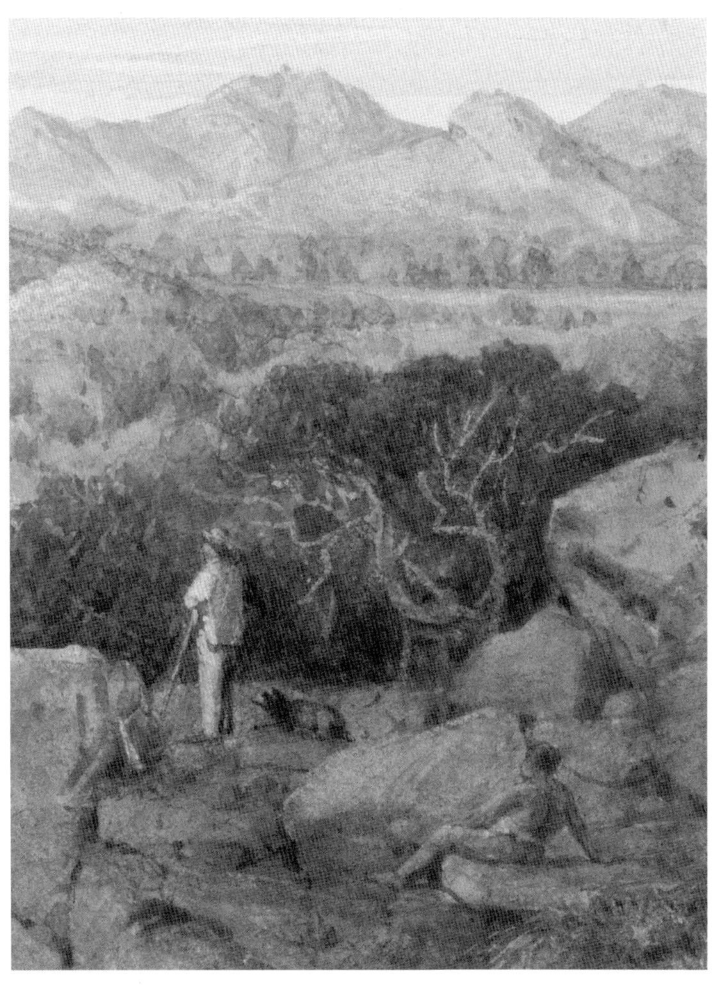

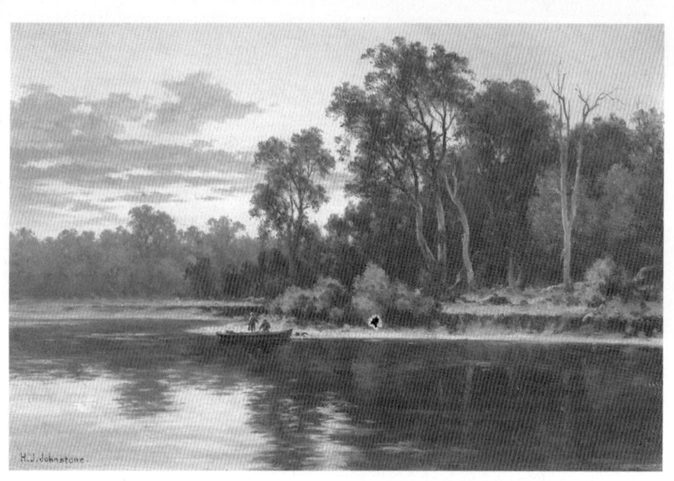
H.J. Johnstone.

HENRY JAMES JOHNSTONE
England / Australia
born Birmingham, England, 1835
died London, England, 1907
Twilight on the Murray 1881
unknown river country, south-east Australia
oil on canvas
20.5 × 30.6 cm
Gift of Barbara Auld 2007
Art Gallery of South Australia, Adelaide
20078P39

Several trees were carefully examined for the thickness of the bark—the gumtree is nourished entirely by the sap running through the bark.

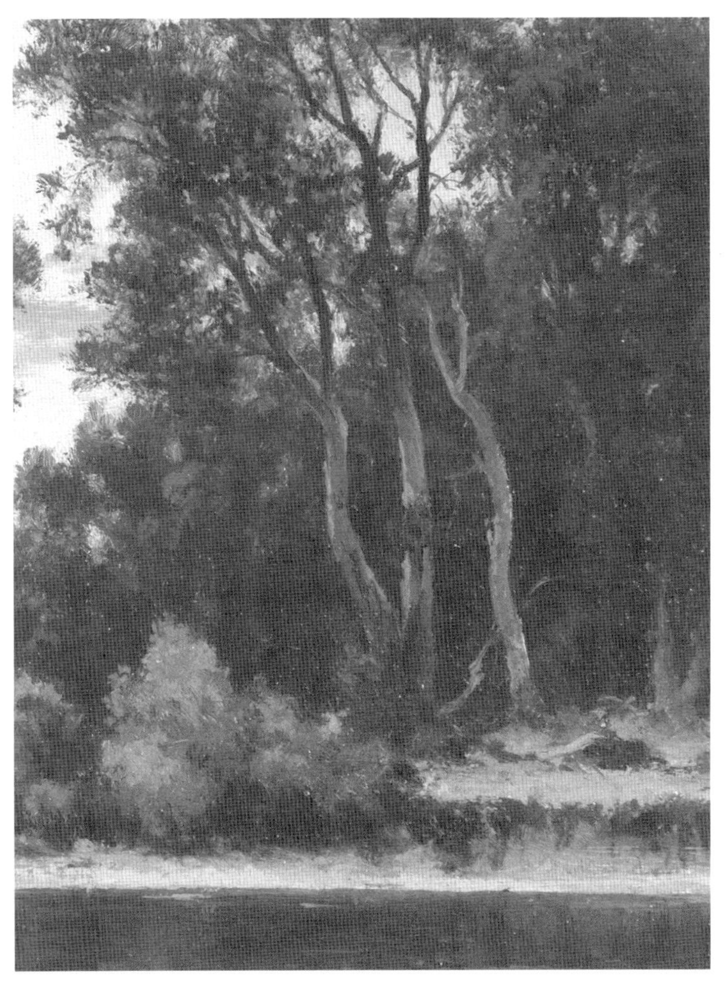

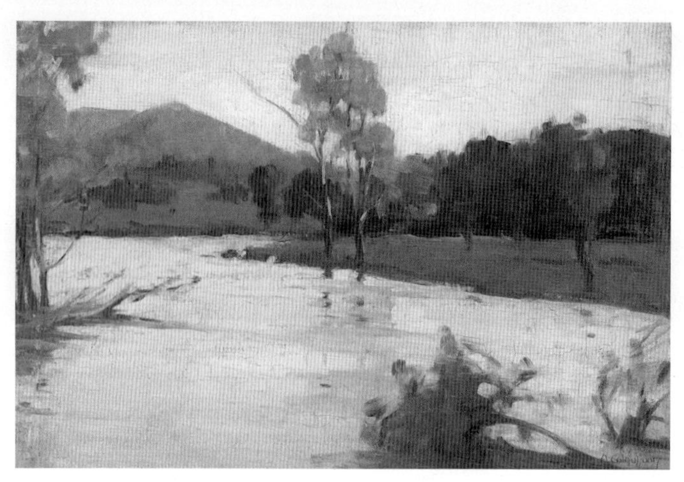

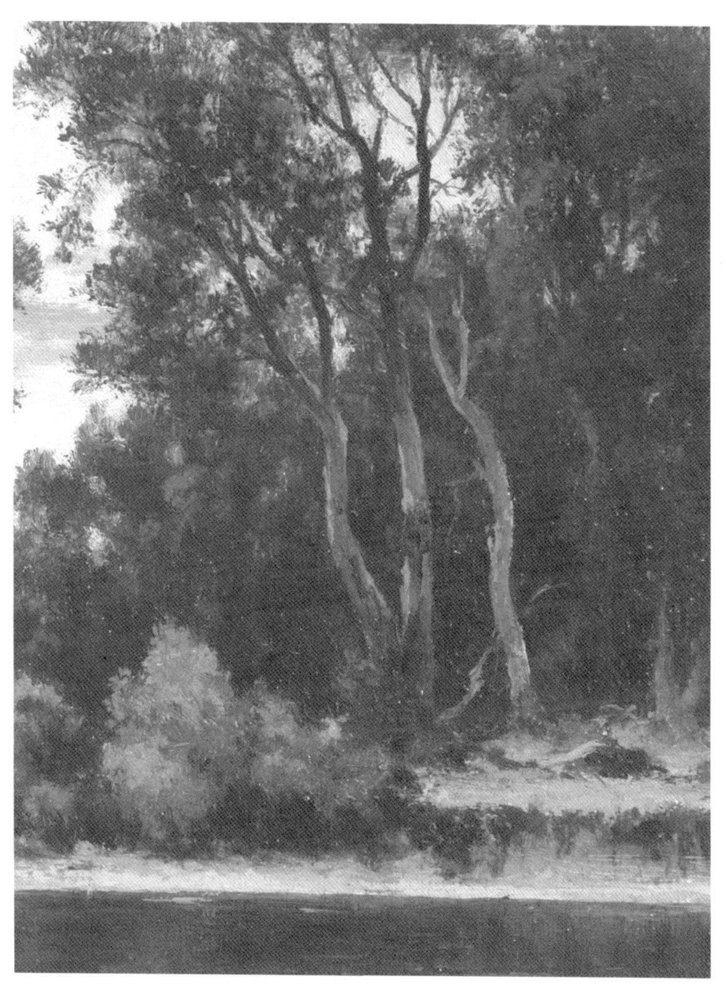

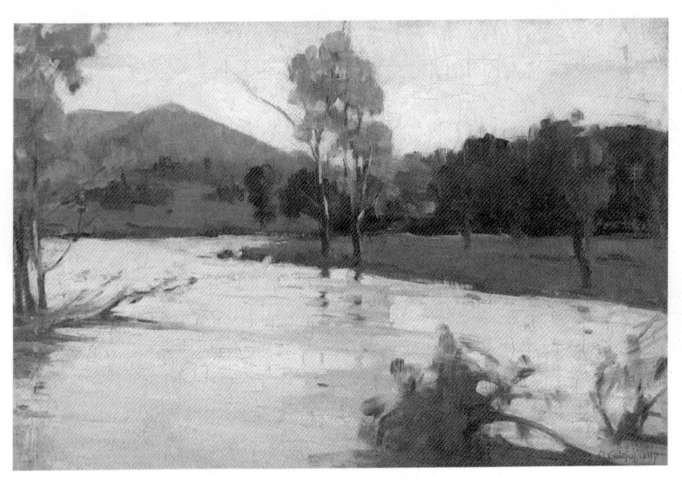

ALEXANDER COLQUHOUN
Scotland / Australia
born Glasgow, Scotland, 1862
died Melbourne, Australia, 1941
The Murray in flood c. 1920
Yorta Yorta country, Victoria
oil on canvas
34.5 × 52.2 cm
Elizabeth and Tom Hunter Bequest 2009
Art Gallery of South Australia, Adelaide
20093P9

The centre of the tree may be burnt by bush fires,

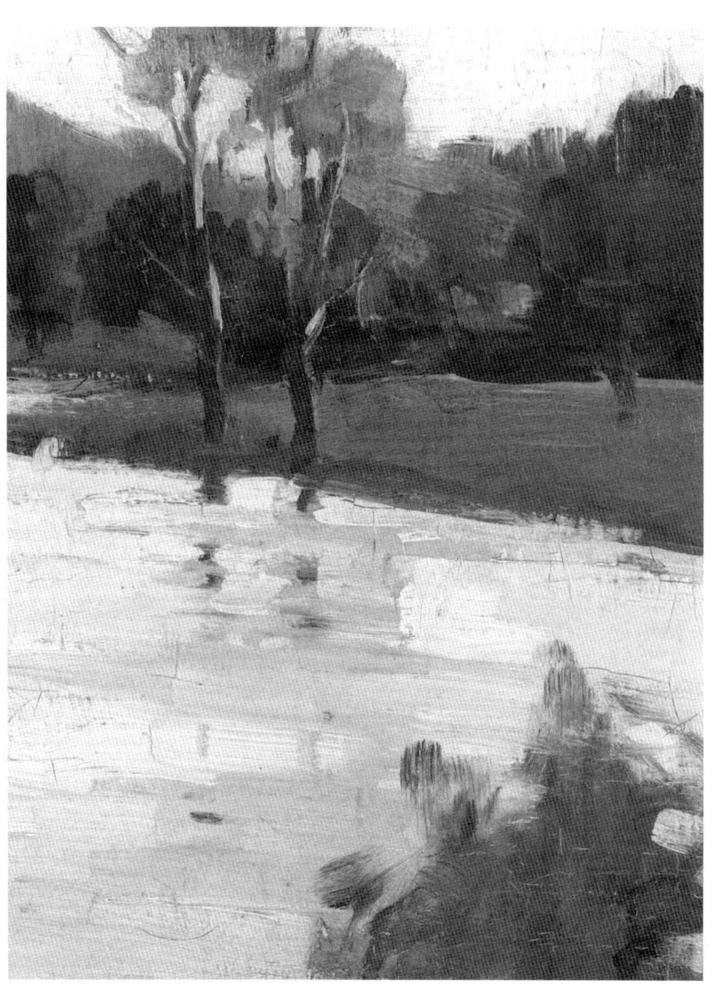

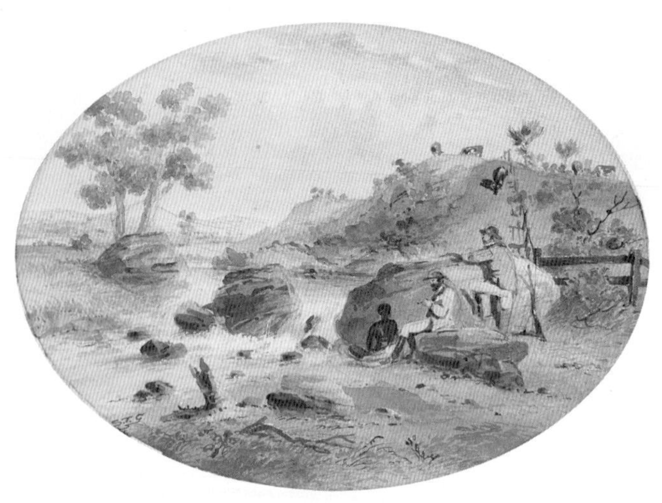

SAMUEL THOMAS GILL
England / Australia
born Perriton, Somerset, England, 1818
died Melbourne, Australia, 1880
Landscape c. 1868
Djadjawurung country, Victoria
watercolour, pen, brush and brown ink, some pencil
19.5 × 27.5 cm
Gift of Miss L.K. Symon 1966
Art Gallery of South Australia, Adelaide
0.2067

but so long as a strip of bark remains there will be foliage.

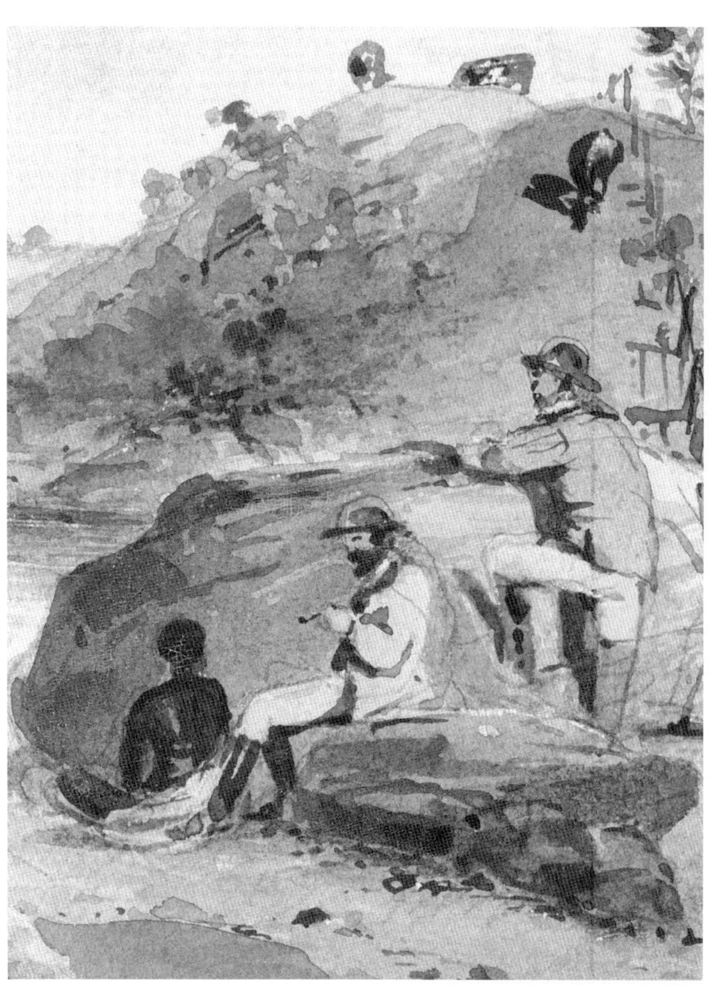

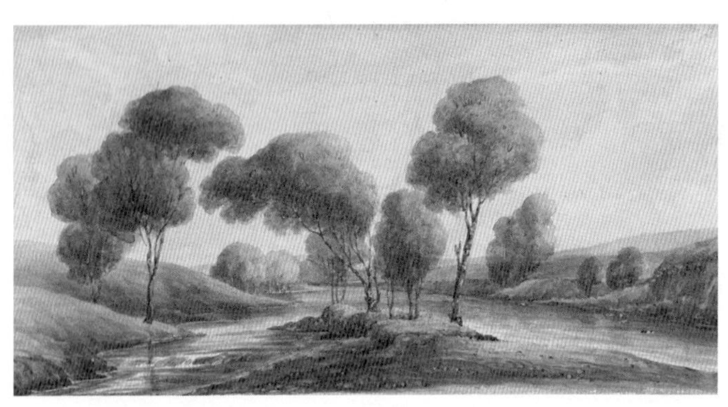

EDWARD CHARLES FROME
England / Australia
born Gibraltar, England, 1802
died Ewell, Surrey, England, 1890
Pasmore River 1843
Danggali country, South Australia
watercolour on paper
13.8 × 27.9 cm
South Australian Government Grant Adelaide City Council and Public Donations 1970
Art Gallery of South Australia, Adelaide
709HP11

The gumtrees along the banks of the Murray were well nurtured owing to their roots being watered sometimes by the overflow of the river, and always by the dampness of the soil a short depth below the surface; consequently the bark was much thicker on some trees than others, and therefore unserviceable for making a canoe.

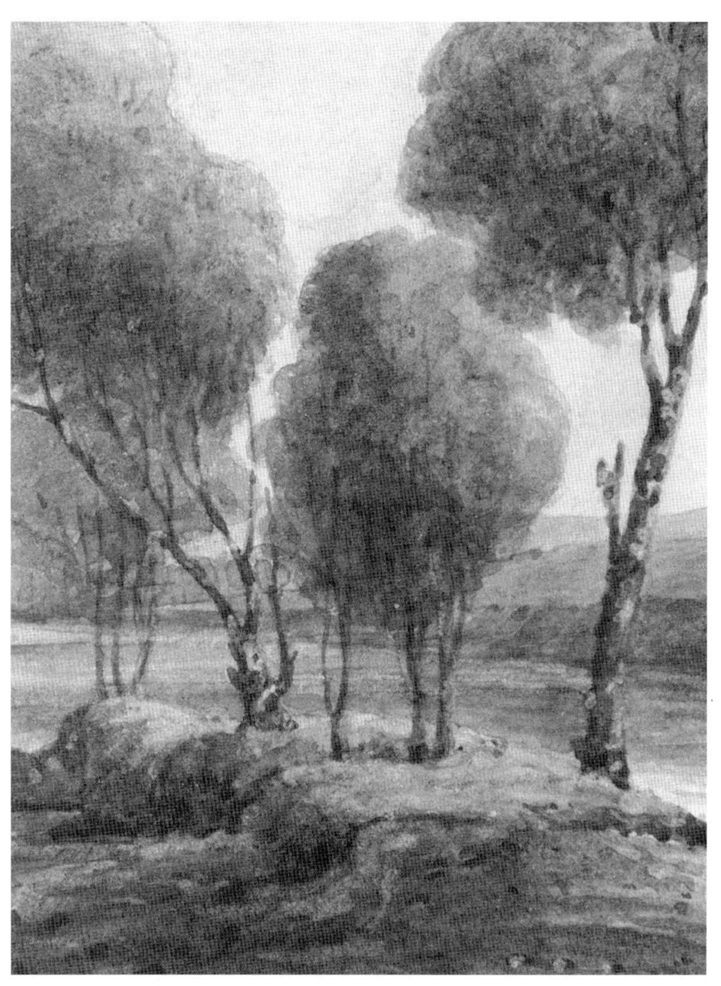

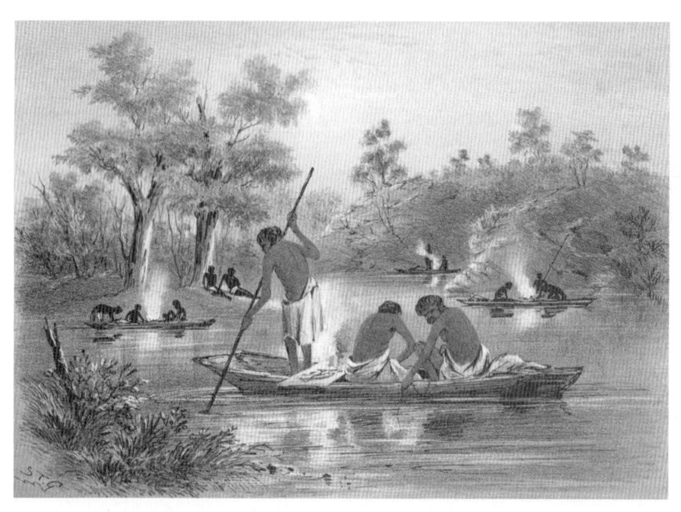

SAMUEL THOMAS GILL
England / Australia
born Perriton, Somerset, England, 1818
died Melbourne, Australia, 1880
Night fishing
plate 19 from *The Australian Sketchbook* 1865, published by Hamel and Ferguson, Melbourne, Australia
unknown river country, south-east Australia
colour lithograph on paper
17.7 × 25.3 cm
South Australian Government Grant 1958
Art Gallery of South Australia, Adelaide
582G28

In testing a tree the native took a yam stick, made of hardwood with a flat point.

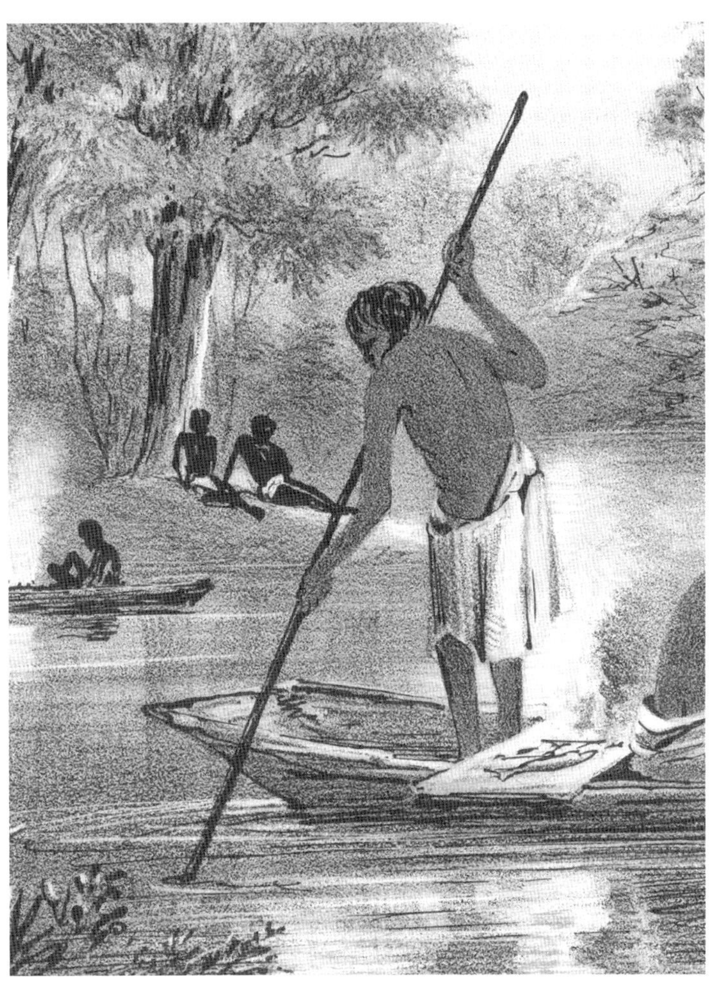

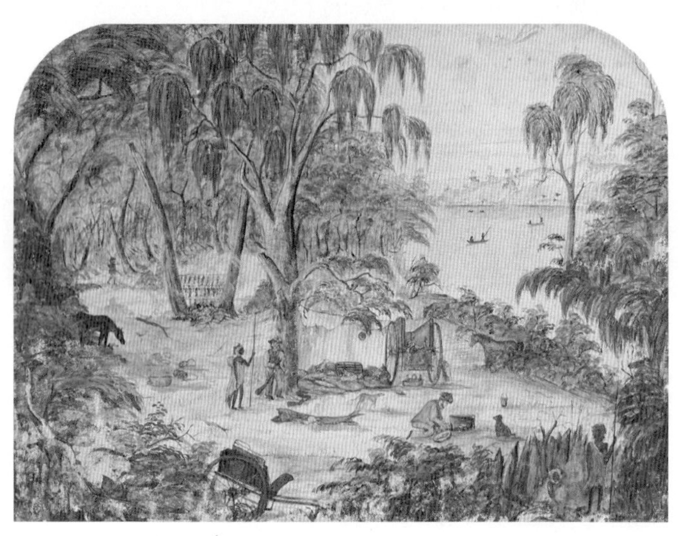

H. MASSEY
Australia
unknown river country, south-east Australia
watercolour
40.4 × 54.5 cm
Transferred from the South Australian Archives 1948, from the Estate of G.V. Ware
Art Gallery of South Australia, Adelaide
721IHP5

With this he began making cuts in the bark for his toes, and also to hold on by when using his yam stick; and by this process he went up trees not only for canoe-making, but also for birds' eggs or opossums. Having found a suitable tree, he, when about 20 ft from the ground, commenced cutting the shape of the canoe through the bark to the hard wood, with his yam stick. This process completed, a rope was passed round the tree, taking about the centre of the canoe. This was to prevent the piece of bark from slipping off before the proper time, in which case a smash would be inevitable.

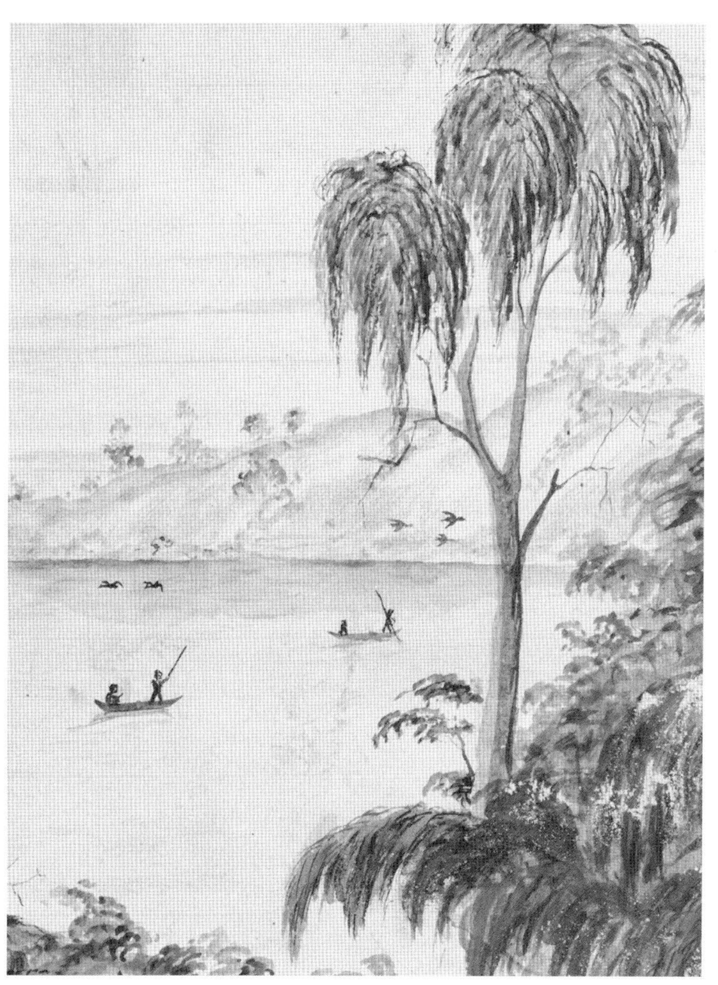

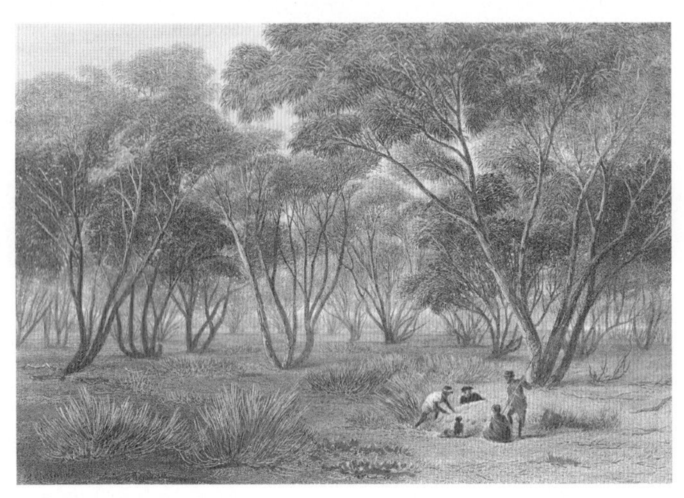

WILLIAM FORREST
Scotland / England
born Edinburgh, Scotland, 1805
died 1889
after NICHOLAS CHEVALIER
Australia / New Zealand
born St Petersburg, Russia, 1828
died London, England, 1902
Mallee scrub, River Murray c. 1870
unknown river country, south-east Australia
engraving, hand-coloured
12.1 × 18.4 cm
David Murray Bequest Fund 1962
Art Gallery of South Australia, Adelaide
563G13

The next proceeding was a ticklish one, and the fate of the canoe depended on the care bestowed on it.

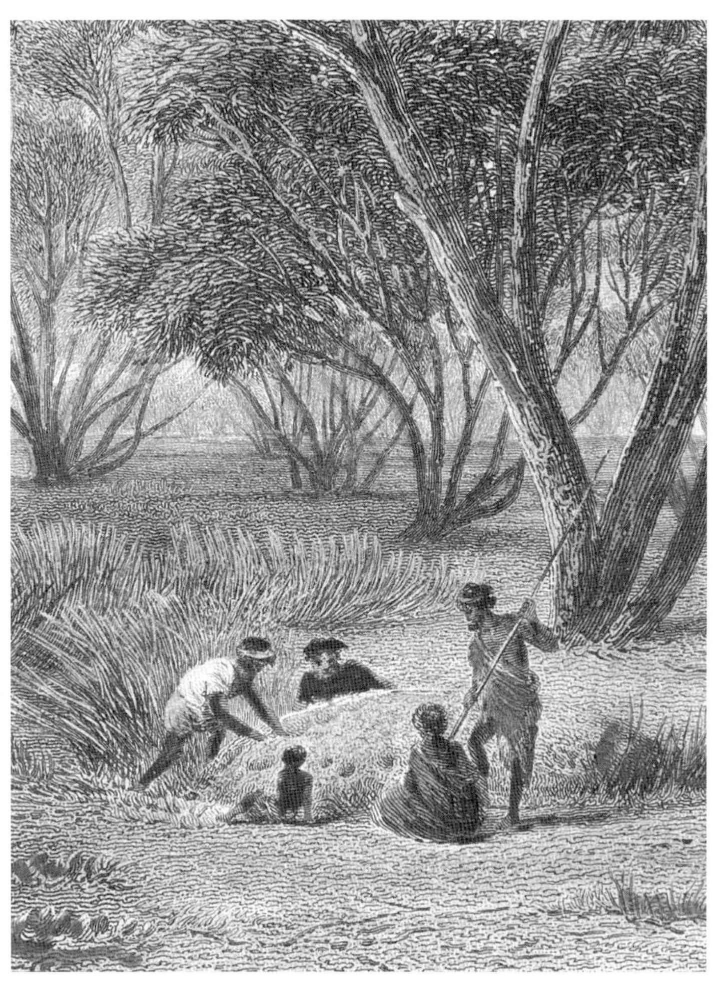

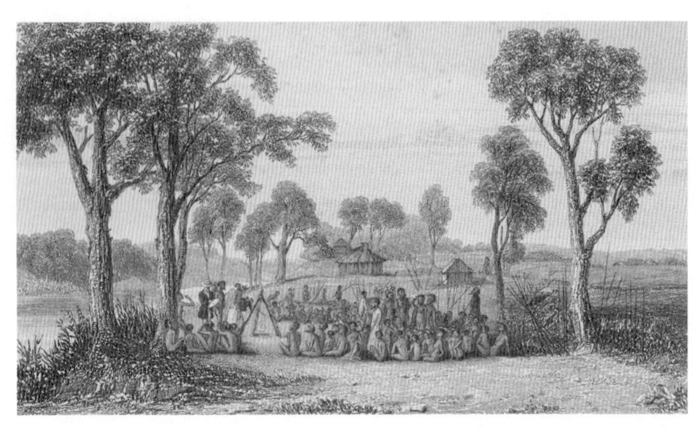

attributed to JOHN HENRY LE KEUX
England
born London, England, 1812
died Durham, England, 1896
after GEORGE HAMILTON
England / Australia
born Hertfordshire, England, 1812
died Adelaide, Australia, 1883
Distribution of flour at Moorunde
Meru country, South Australia
engraving on paper
9 × 16.1 cm
Art Gallery of South Australia, Adelaide
563G10

Several pliable, thin flat sticks were carefully forced in between the bark and the tree; short spaces apart, but only short distances at a time. When a large canoe was being made a second cord was passed round the tree, so that the canoe should not tip over when separated from the tree.

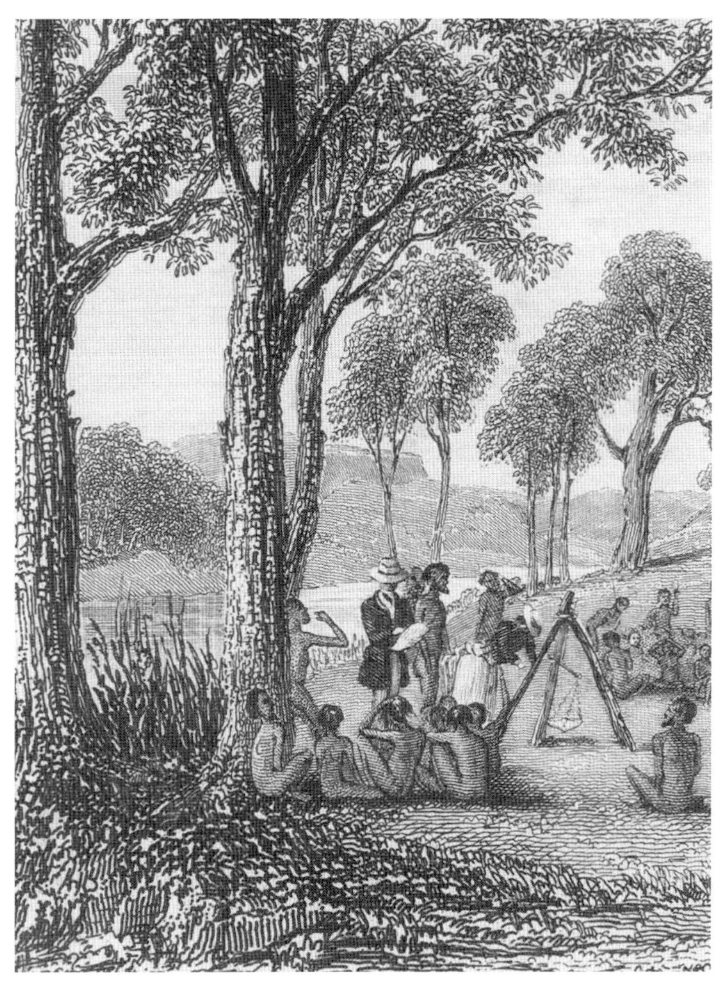

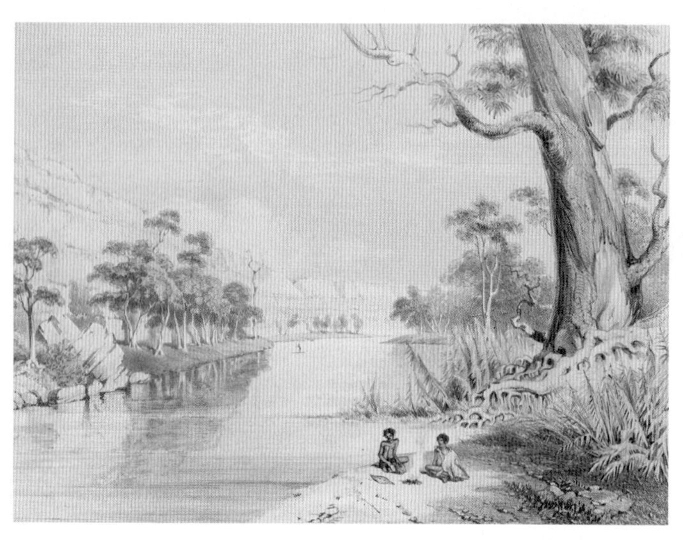

JAMES WILLIAM GILES
Scotland / Italy
born Aberdeen, Scotland, 1801
died Aberdeen, Scotland, 1870
after GEORGE FRENCH ANGAS
England / Australia
born Newcastle-upon-Tyne, England, 1822
died London, England, 1886
The River Murray above Moorundi 1847
Meru country, South Australia
hand-coloured lithograph on paper
23.9 × 32.1 cm
Bequest of Christine Margaret MacGregor 1975
Art Gallery of South Australia, Adelaide
758G68

As soon as the separation was performed the cords were eased so as to allow the canoe to slip down until the lower end rested on the ground, and six or eight natives were ready to receive it as the cords were gradually loosed, and place it flat on the ground.

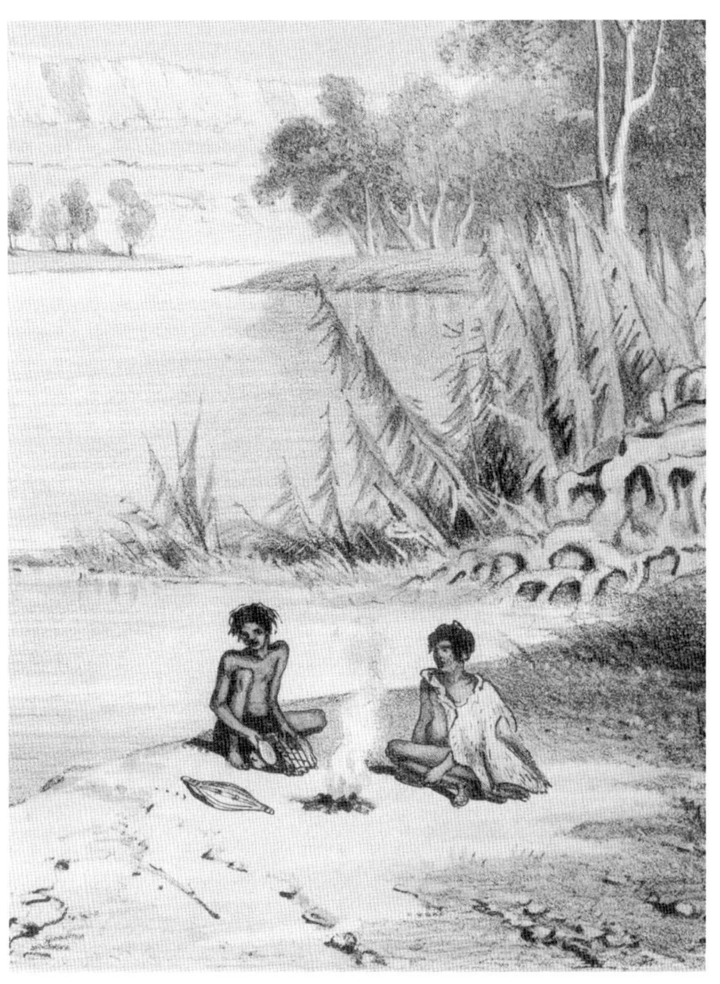

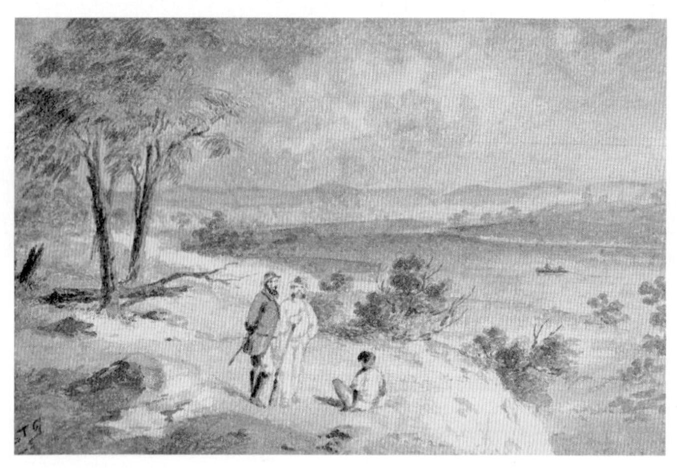

SAMUEL THOMAS GILL
England / Australia
born Perriton, Somerset, England, 1818
died Melbourne, Australia, 1880
Metcalfe's Station, River Murray 1844
Meru country, South Australia
black-and-grey watercolour wash on paper
22.5 × 35.8 cm
South Australian Government Grant 1963
Art Gallery of South Australia, Adelaide
6310D4

Now commenced the manipulation of this great heavy piece of bark into the proper shape for a canoe.

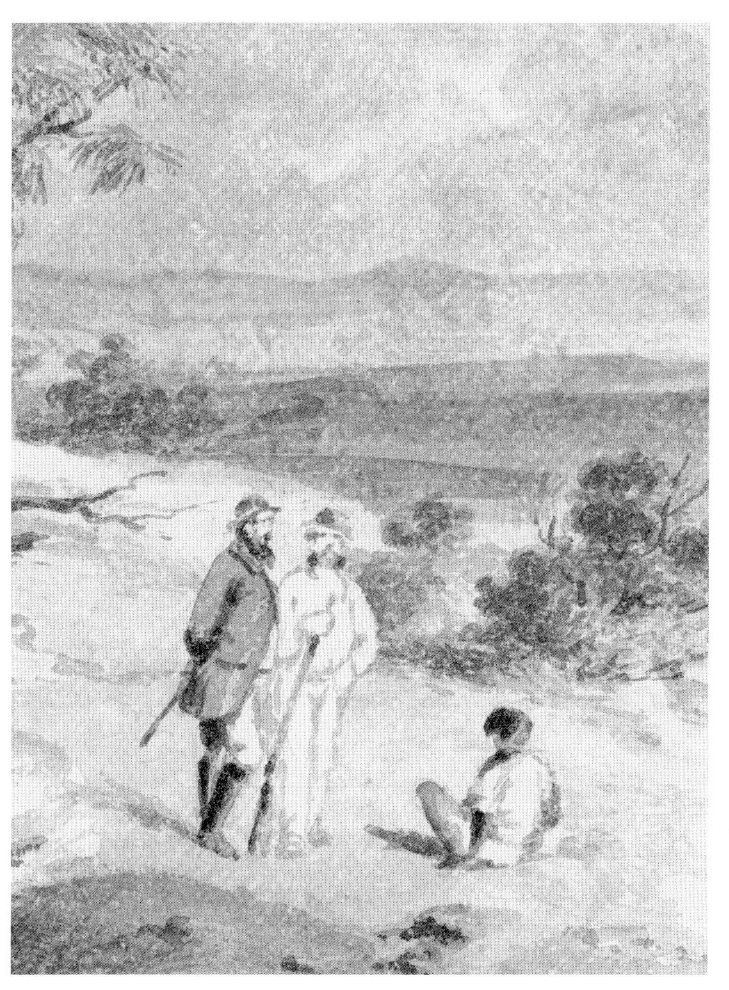

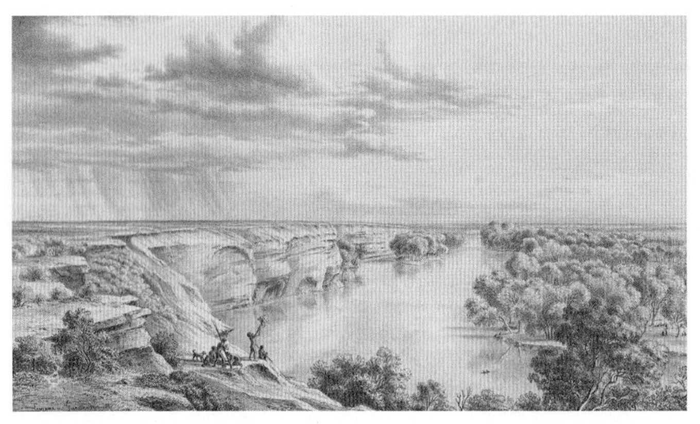

EUGENE VON GUÉRARD
Austria / England / Australia
born Vienna, Austria, 1811
died London, England, 1901
View of the Murray River, South Australia
plate 8 from *Eugene von Guérard's Australian Landscapes* 1866–68, published by Hamel and Ferguson, Melbourne, Australia
Meru country, South Australia
colour lithograph on paper
27.9 × 49.2 cm
Gift of Mr George Holman 1945
Art Gallery of South Australia, Adelaide
4510G30

The bark at the upper end was much thinner than that at the lower end, the latter being nearer the base of the tree.

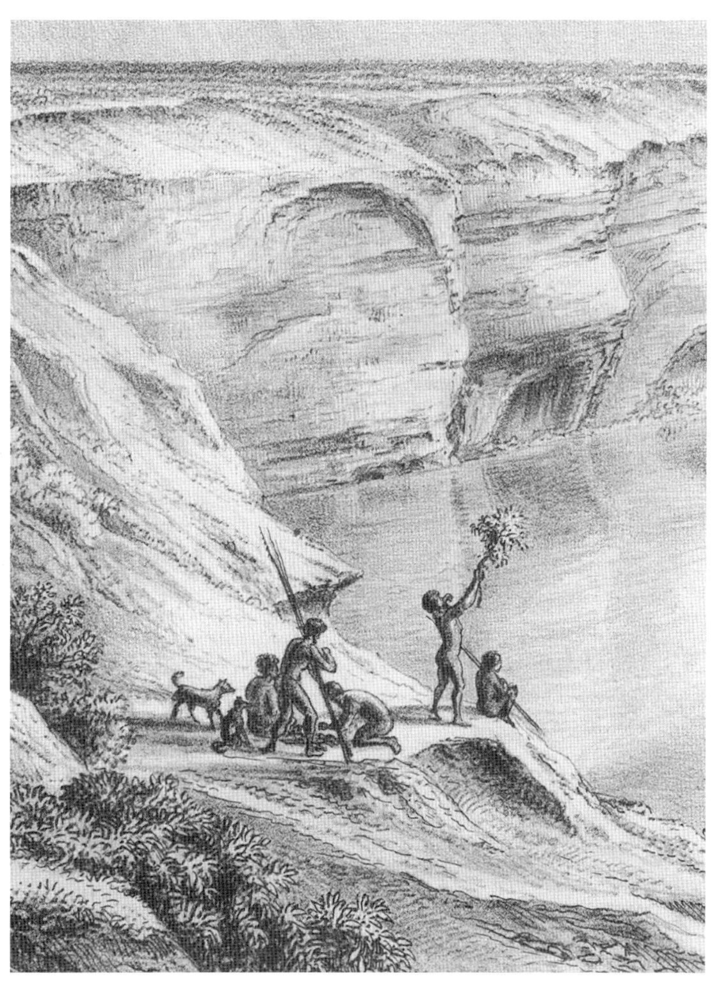

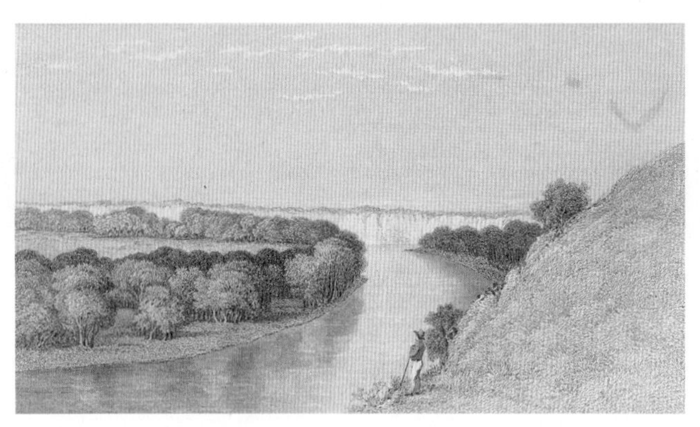

HENRY MELVILLE
England
born 1826
died 1841
The Murray River 1844
Meru country, South Australia
wood engraving on paper
9.5 × 17.2 cm
Bequest of V.K. Burmeister 1957
Art Gallery of South Australia, Adelaide
575G407

Props were now placed under the sides of the canoe, and small fires were made inside at various distances to evaporate a good deal of the sap, and also to cause the sides to curl up sufficiently to keep the water out when afloat, stretchers being put across to prevent too great a curl.

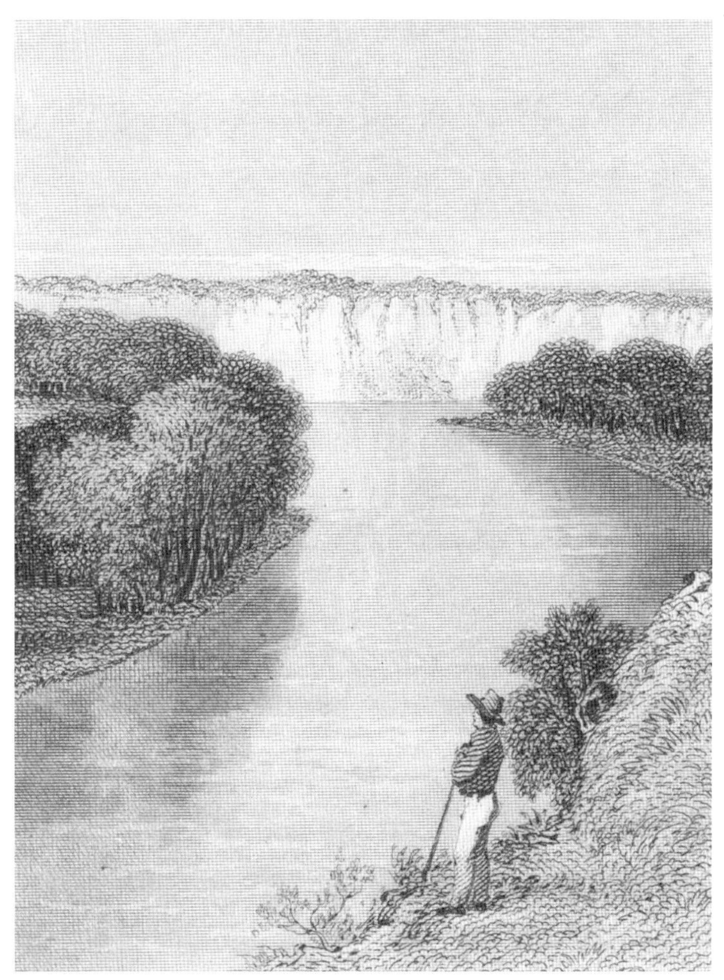

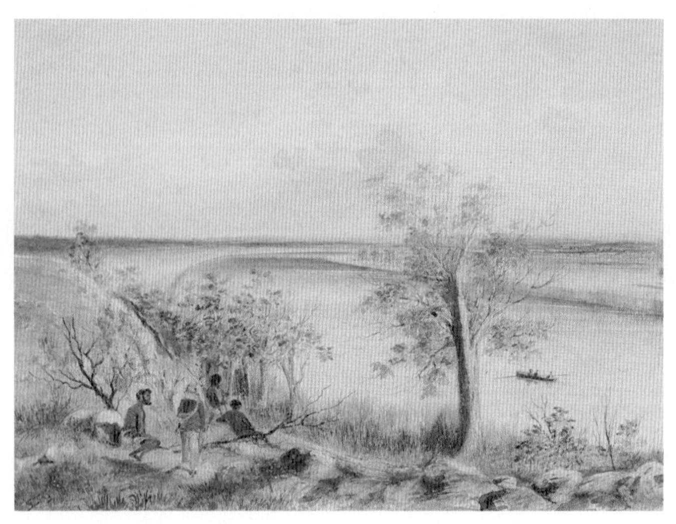

SAMUEL THOMAS GILL
England / Australia
born Perriton, Somerset, England, 1818
died Melbourne, Australia, 1880
River Murray scene
Ngarrindjeri country, South Australia
watercolour
24.2 × 37.2 cm
Grant for the Purchase of South Australian Historical Items
Art Gallery of South Australia, Adelaide
0.1910

Much care had to be used in the drying and curling process, as too great or sudden heat would split the bark and render it useless, but this seldom happened.

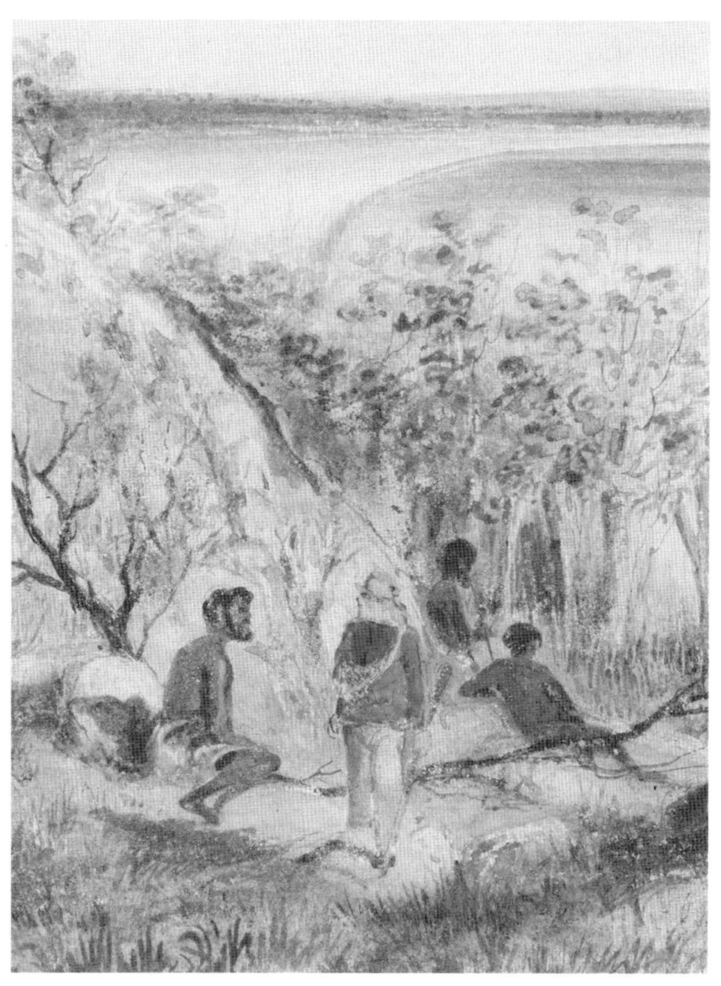

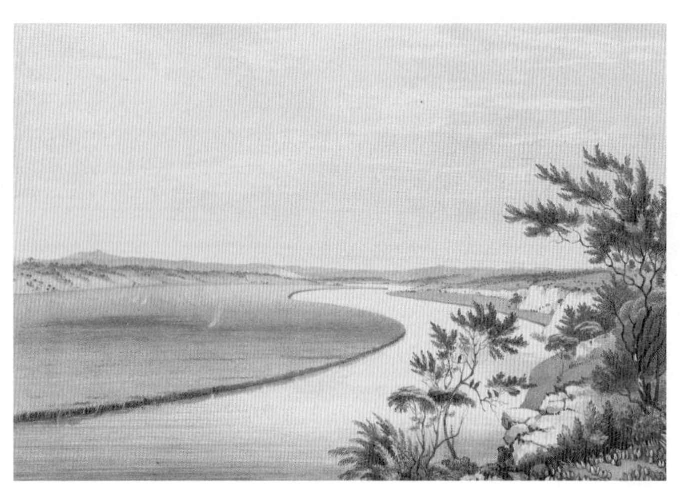

JAMES WILLIAM GILES
Scotland / Italy
born Aberdeen, Scotland, 1801
died Aberdeen, Scotland, 1870
after GEORGE FRENCH ANGAS
England / Australia
born Newcastle-upon-Tyne, England, 1822
died London, England, 1886
The River Murray near Lake Alexandrina
plate 25 from *South Australia Illustrated* 1847,
London, England
Ngarrindjeri country, South Australia
colour lithograph on paper
23.2 × 32 cm
Gift of Mr Keith Angas 1945
Art Gallery of South Australia, Adelaide
455G15

The thin bark at the upper end was made the bow, and bent well up, while the thick bark at the lower end represented the stern, and this could not be curled.

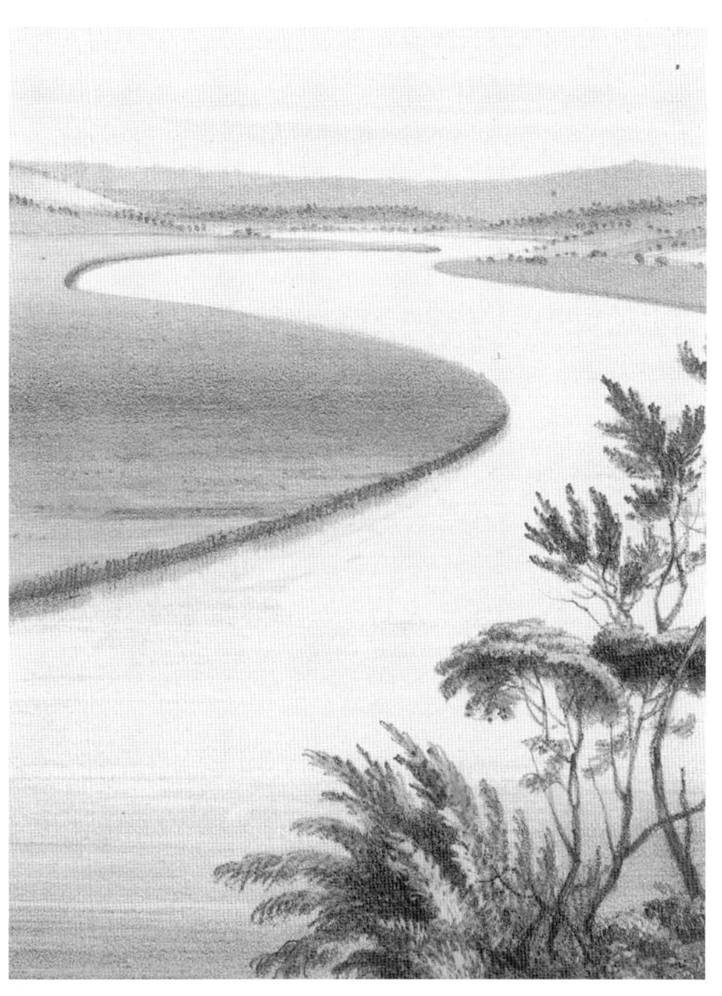

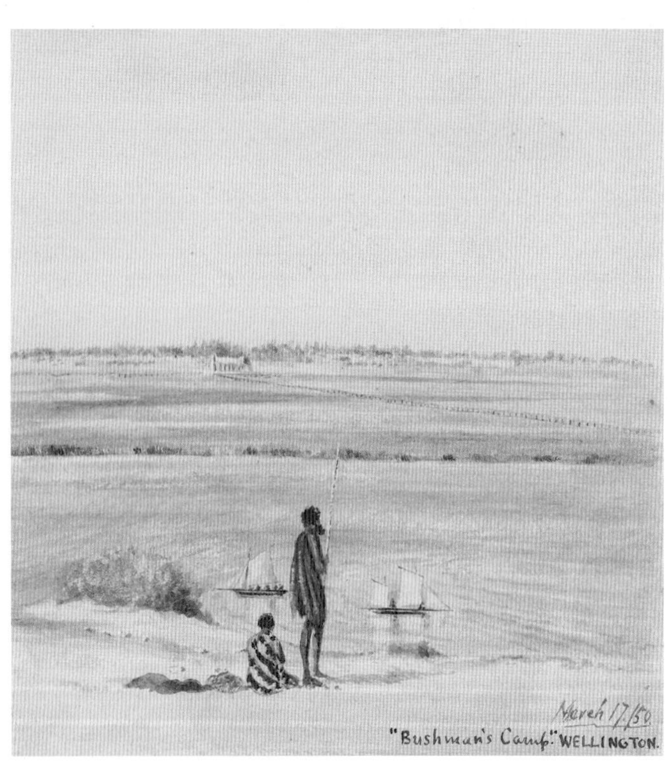
March 17/50
"Bushman's Camp." WELLINGTON.

JOHN MICHAEL SKIPPER
England / Australia
born Norwich, England, 1815
died Adelaide, Australia, 1883
Bushman's camp, Wellington, South Australia 1850
Ngarrindjeri country, Wellington, South Australia
watercolour on paper
13 × 12.1 cm
Morgan Thomas Bequest Fund 1942
Art Gallery of South Australia, Adelaide
0.1218

In order, therefore, to keep the water out a mass of clay from the river bank, well mixed with grass to bind it, was put as a barricade against the water; and if renewed occasionally it served the purpose very well.

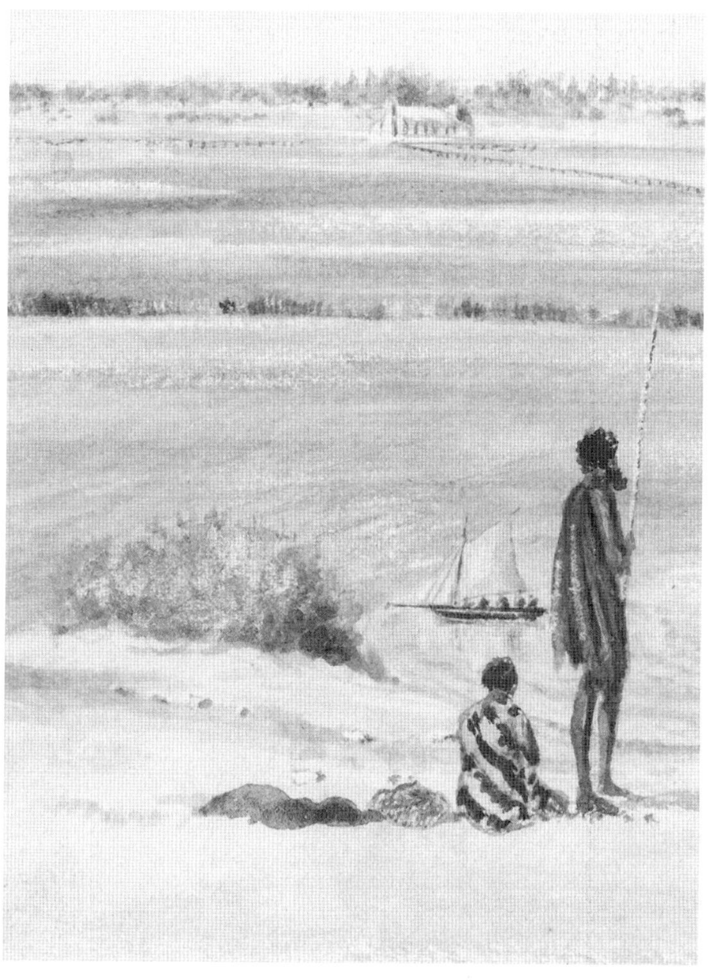

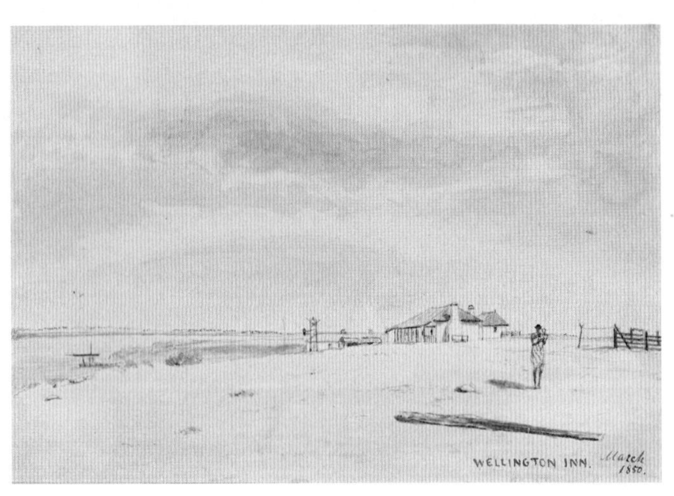
WELLINGTON INN.
March
1850.

JOHN MICHAEL SKIPPER
England / Australia
born Norwich, England, 1815
died Adelaide, Australia, 1883
Wellington Inn 1850
Ngarrindjeri country, Wellington, South Australia
watercolour on paper
12.2 × 17.6 cm
Morgan Thomas Bequest Fund 1942
Art Gallery of South Australia, Adelaide
0.1207

Several days were required before the canoe was sufficiently dry to put in the water, and even then the weight was so great that several natives had to drag it down to the river; but when once launched it lasted for a considerable period.

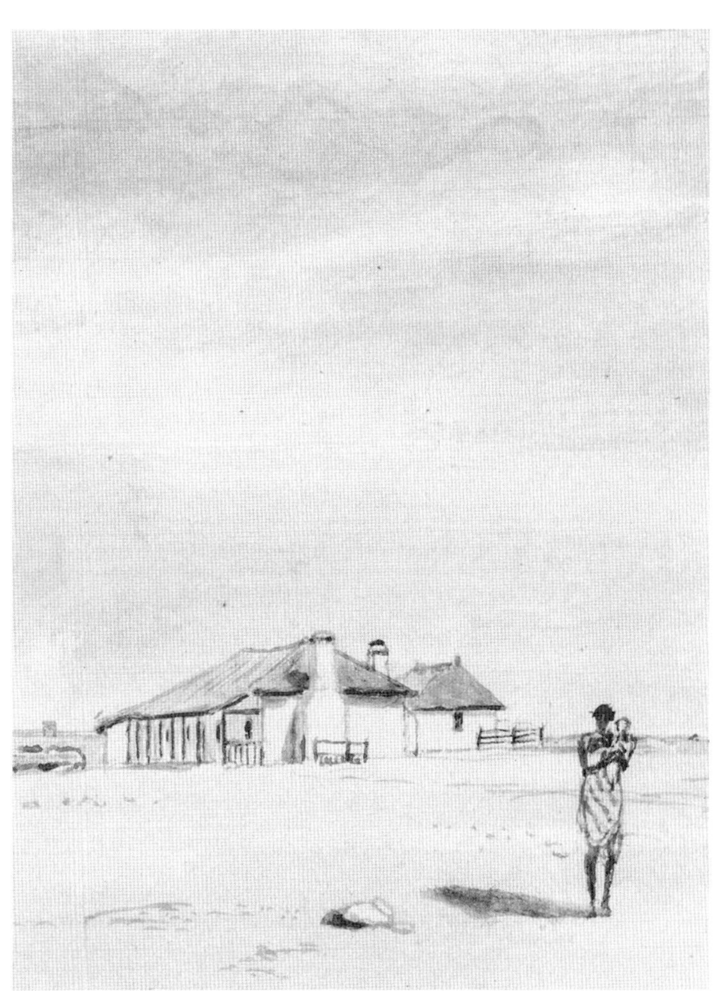

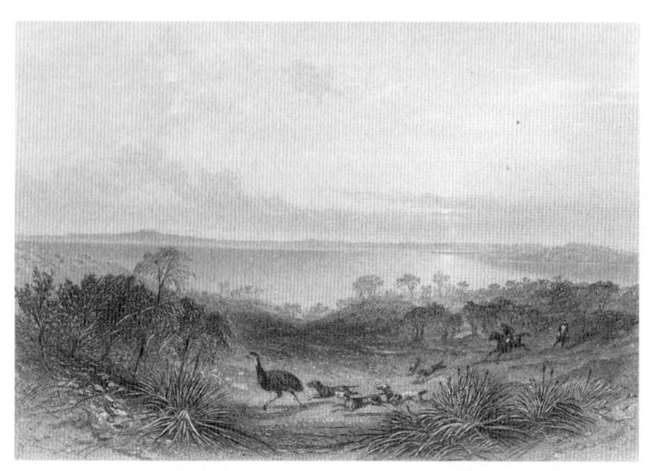

ARTHUR WILLMORE
England
born Birmingham, England, 1814
died England 1888
after SAMUEL PROUT
England / Australia
born Plymouth, England, 1783
died London, England, 1852
Lake Albert
Ngarrindjeri country, South Australia
steel engraving on paper
12.3 × 18.2 cm
Art Gallery of South Australia, Adelaide
5710G510

To propel the canoe a thinned sapling fir tree about fourteen feet in length was used, to one end of which were attached two sharp mallee-wood prongs for the purpose of spearing fish, one prong being a little longer than the other.

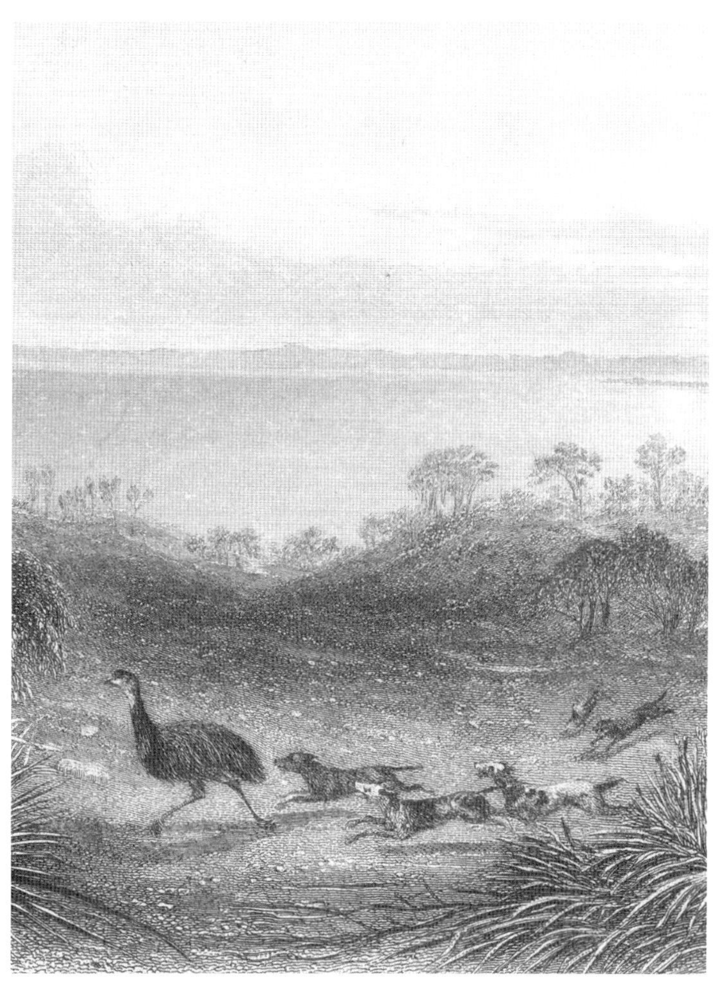

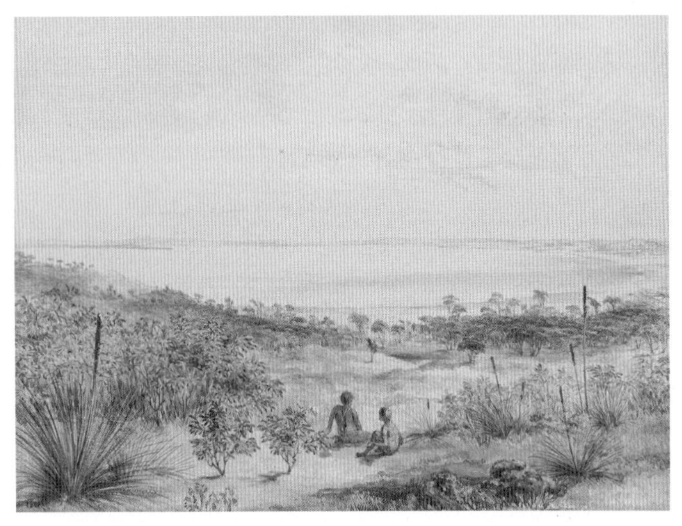

GEORGE FRENCH ANGAS
England / Australia
born Newcastle-upon-Tyne, England, 1822
died London, England, 1886
Lake Albert 1844
Ngarrindjeri country, South Australia
watercolour on paper
24.7 × 34 cm
Bequest of J. Angas Johnson 1902
Art Gallery of South Australia, Adelaide
0.617

This end of the pole was also employed for paddling, while the other served to push the canoe along when in shallow water.

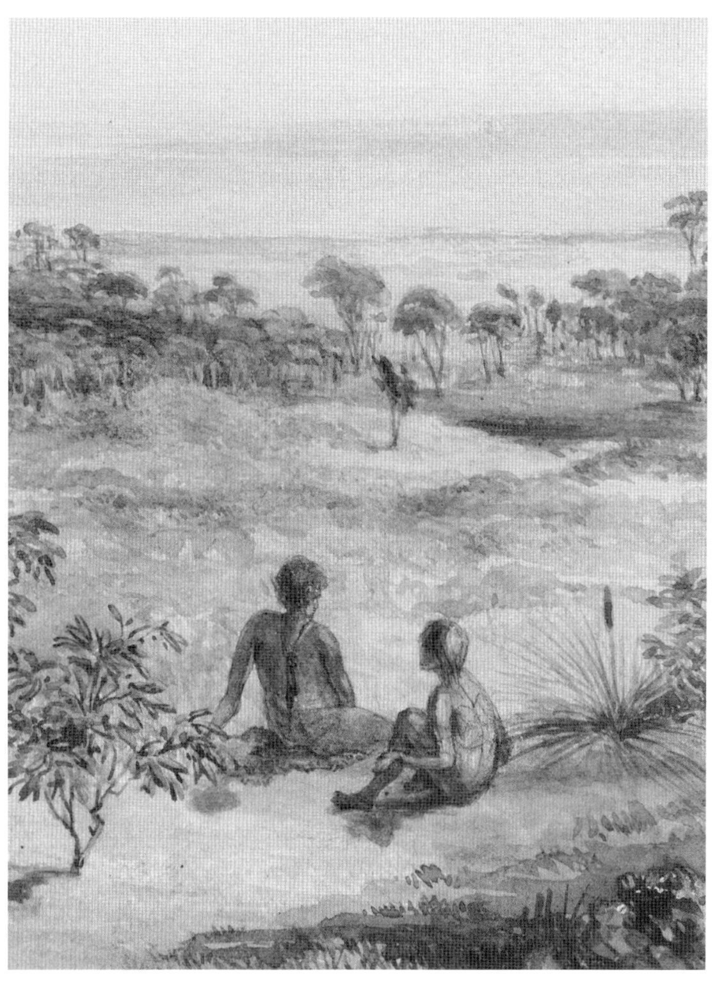

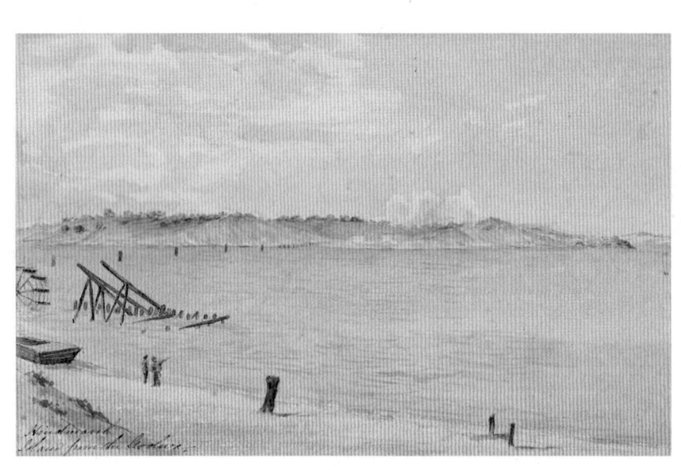

RICHARD ERNEST MINCHIN
Ireland / Australia
born Tipperary, Ireland, 1831
died Mount Barker, South Australia, 1893
Hindmarsh Island from Goolwa c. mid-1850s–1890
Ngarrindjeri country, Goolwa, South Australia
watercolour on paper
8.9 × 15.2 cm
Morgan Thomas Bequest Fund 1938
Art Gallery of South Australia, Adelaide
0.956

In cold weather a clay coating was put on a small space in the bottom of the canoe, and a fire was lit for warmth.

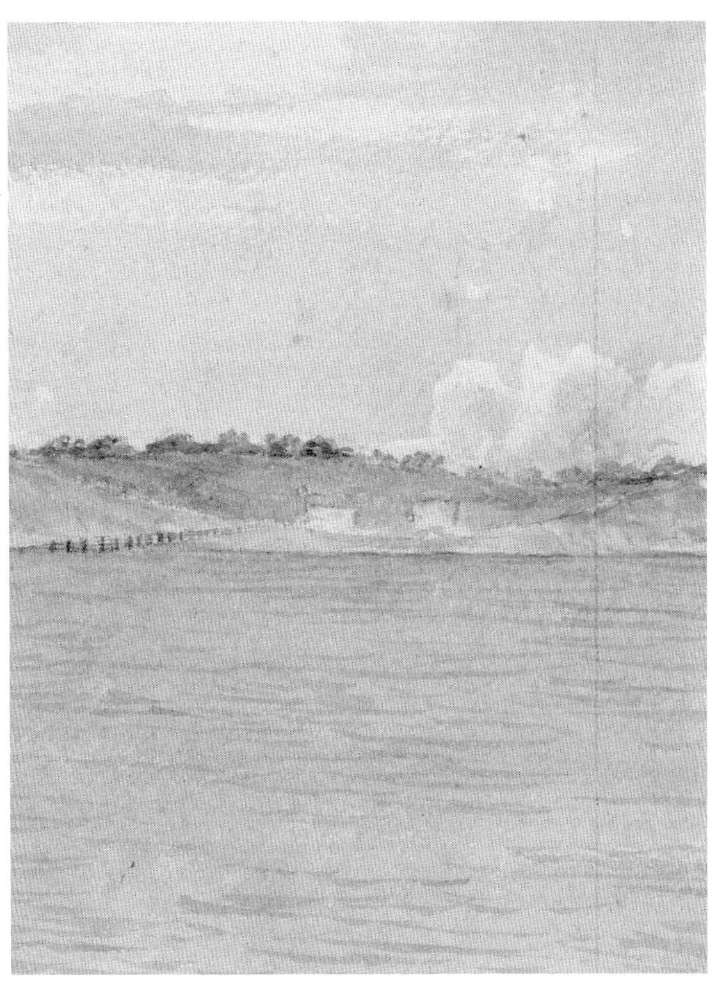

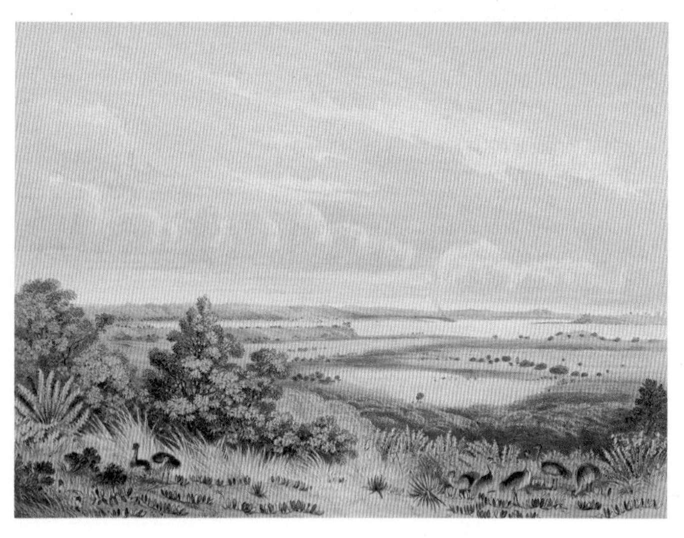

JAMES WILLIAM GILES
Scotland / Italy
born Aberdeen, Scotland, 1801
died Aberdeen, Scotland, 1870
after GEORGE FRENCH ANGAS
England / Australia
born Newcastle-upon-Tyne, England, 1822
died London, England, 1886
The Goolwa with part of Hindmarsh Island c. 1847
Ngarrindjeri country, Goolwa, South Australia
hand-coloured lithograph on paper
25.9 × 35.5 cm
South Australian Government Grant 1953
Art Gallery of South Australia, Adelaide
533G48

The ropes used for holding the craft to the tree were made by the natives from a very fibrous grass, and so were all the cord and the twine for making their nets.

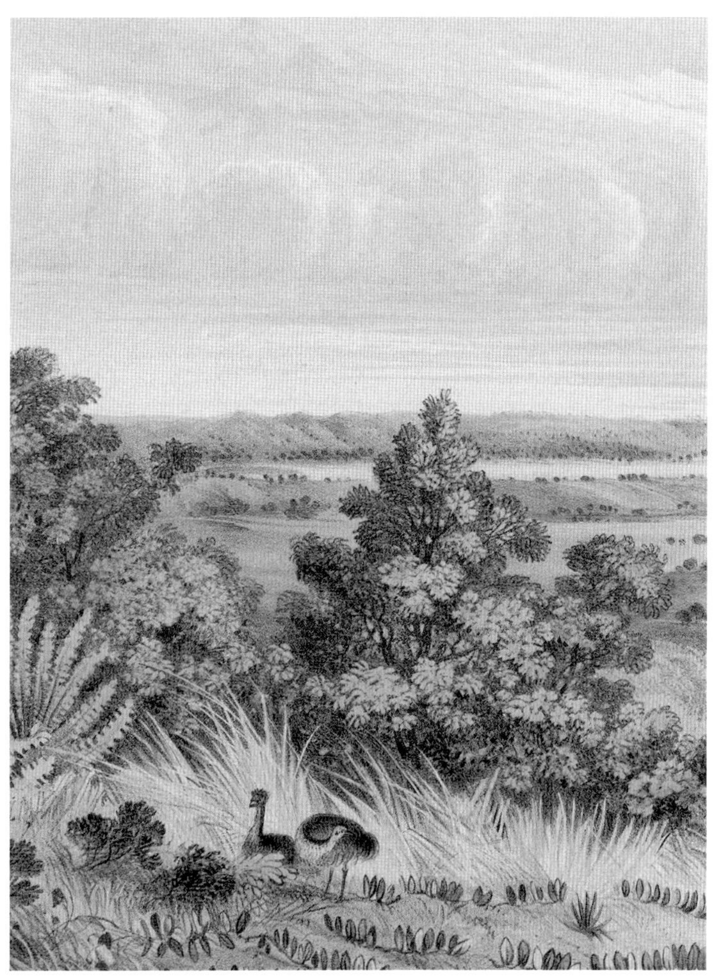

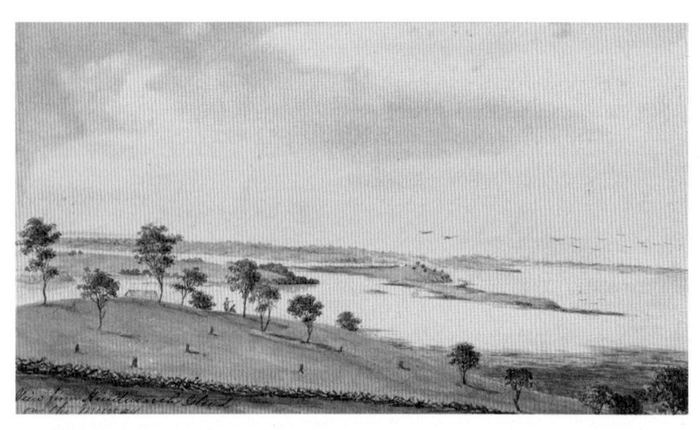

RICHARD ERNEST MINCHIN
Ireland / Australia
born Tipperary, Ireland, 1831
died Mount Barker, South Australia, 1893
View from Hindmarsh Island on the Murray
c. mid-1850s–1890
Ngarrindjeri country, Hindmarsh Island, South Australia
watercolour on paper
15.2 × 26.3 cm
Morgan Thomas Bequest Fund 1938
Art Gallery of South Australia, Adelaide
0.964

The canoes were about ten to twelve feet in length and two feet six inches in width.

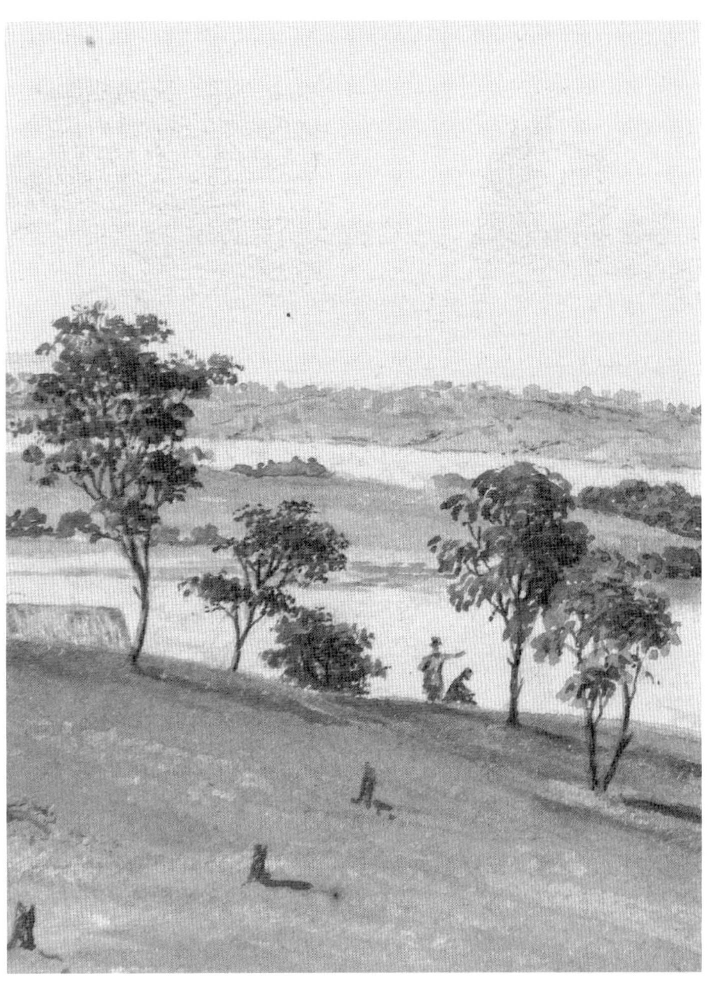

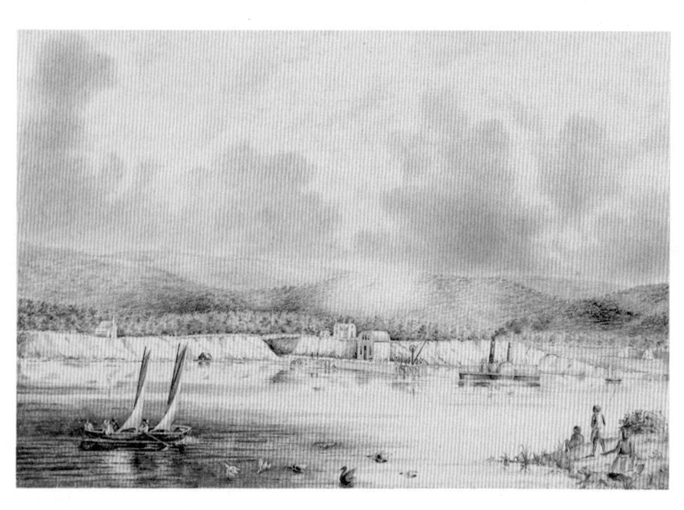

JAMES HAZEL ADAMSON
Scotland / Australia
born Hawick, Scotland, 1829
died Adelaide, Australia, 1902
View of Goolwa with the "Lady Augusta" approaching the jetty 1854
Ngarrindjeri country, Goolwa, South Australia
pencil, brown watercolour wash, white gouache, pen and ink on paper
22.4 × 30.2 cm
Gift of Edward and Sue Tweddell, Michael Hayes and Adam Wynn through the Art Gallery of South Australia Foundation Collectors' Club 2004
Art Gallery of South Australia, Adelaide
20049D6

When making the fires inside to evaporate the sap, great care had to be used to keep the bottom from curling, and to ensure its being quite flat stones were placed to weight it down.

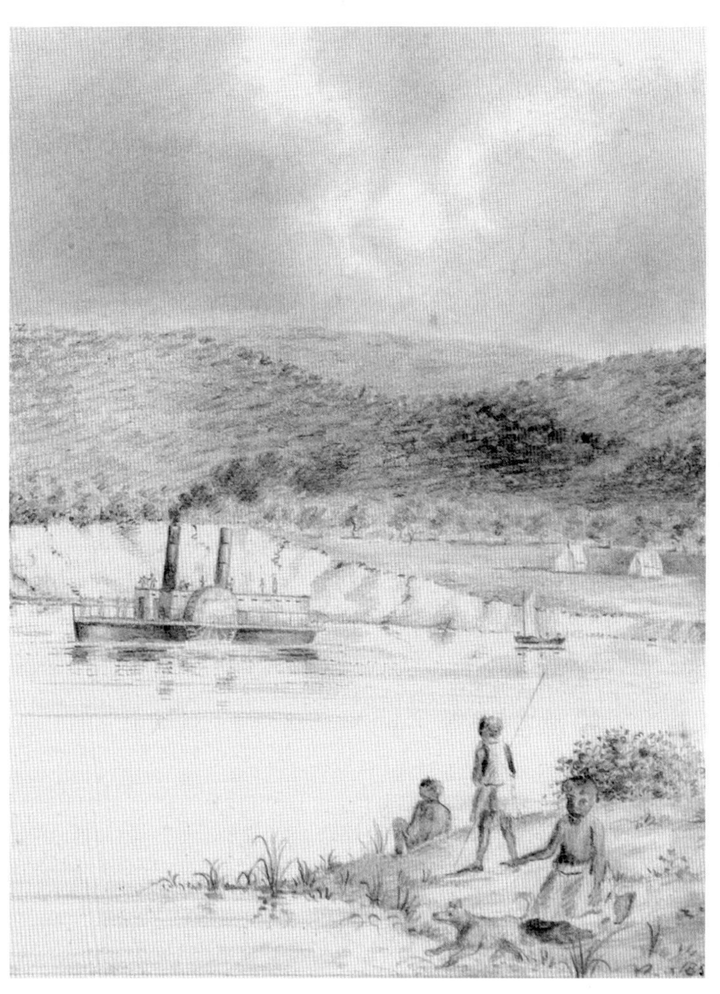

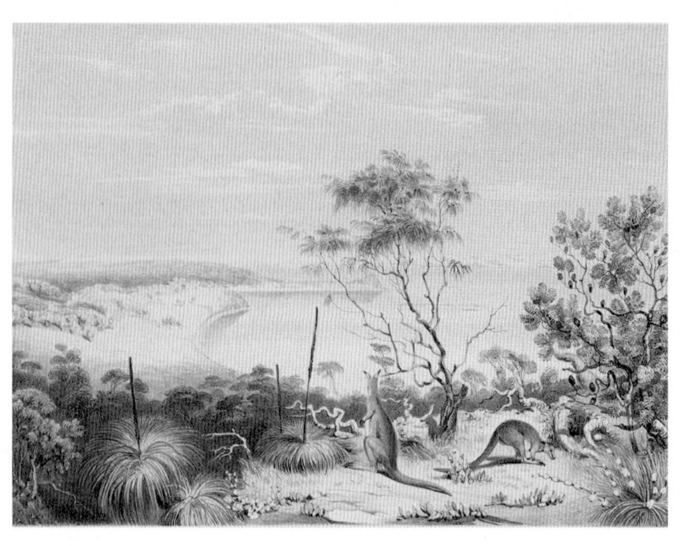

JAMES WILLIAM GILES
Scotland / Italy
born Aberdeen, Scotland, 1801
died Aberdeen, Scotland, 1870
after GEORGE FRENCH ANGAS
England / Australia
born Newcastle-upon-Tyne, England, 1822
died London, England, 1886
Scene on the Coorong, near Lake Albert
Ngarrindjeri country, Coorong, South Australia
hand-coloured lithograph on paper
23.2 × 32.4 cm
South Australian Government Grant 1953
Art Gallery of South Australia, Adelaide
533G9

The canoe to a Murray River native was as useful as a vehicle to a white man.

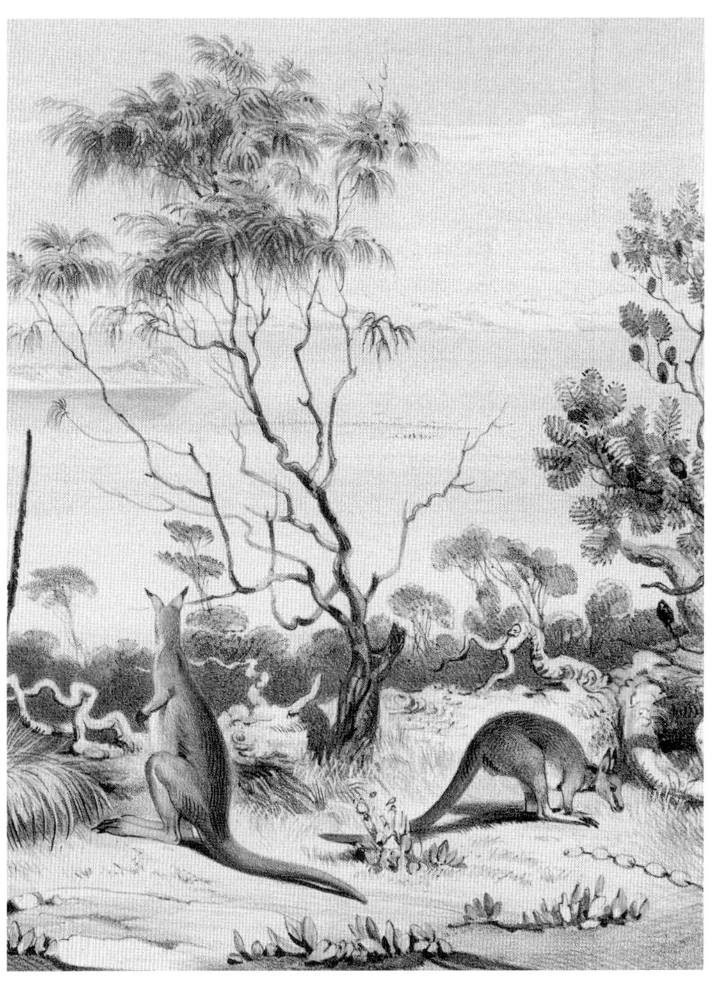

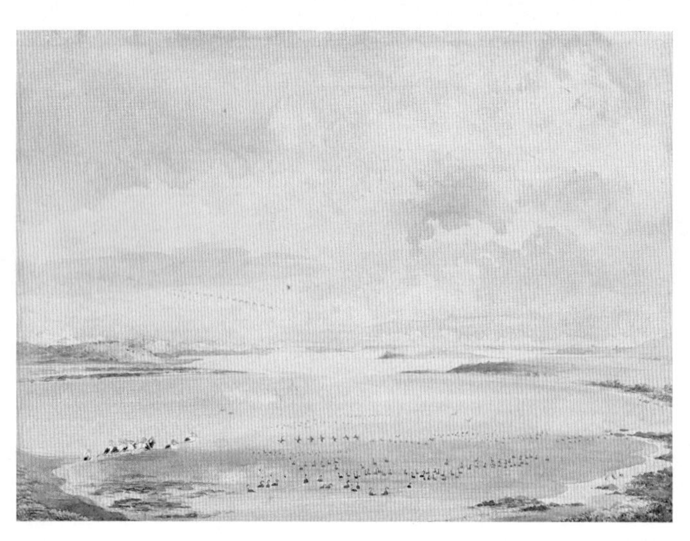

GEORGE FRENCH ANGAS
England / Australia
born Newcastle-upon-Tyne, England, 1822
died London, England, 1886
Scene on the Coorong 1844
Ngarrindjeri country, Coorong, South Australia
watercolour and gouache on paper
26 × 35.8 cm
Bequest of J. Angas Johnson 1902
Art Gallery of South Australia, Adelaide
0.622

By its means he was able to move his family and small belongings to many localities along the river, as well as frequently provide sustenance for himself and them by fishing with lines and spearing fish in shallow lagoons.

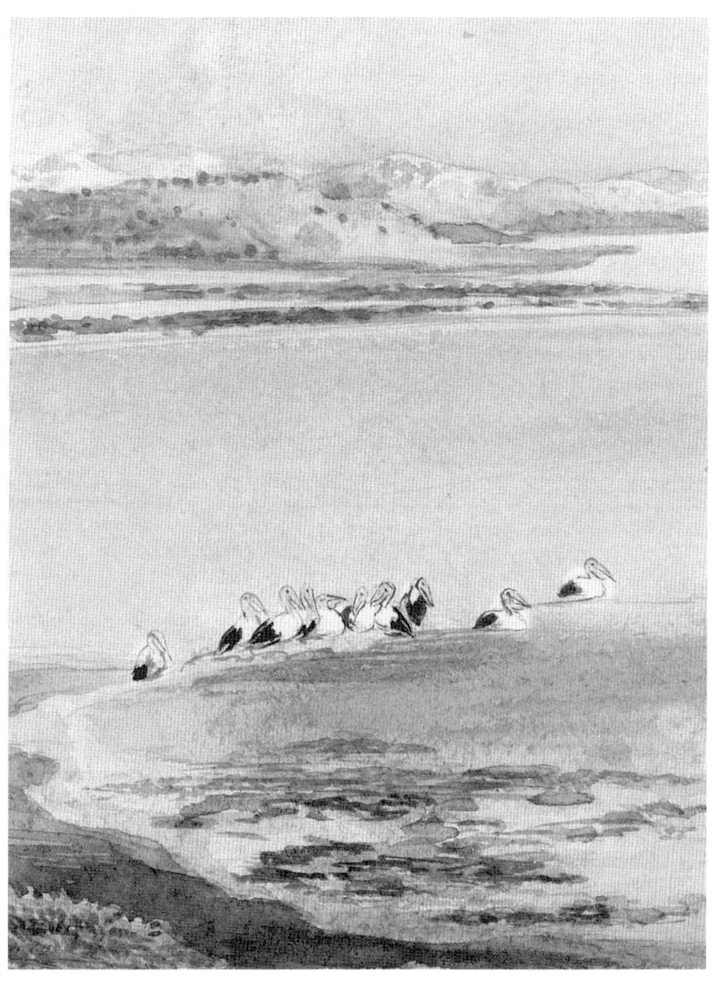

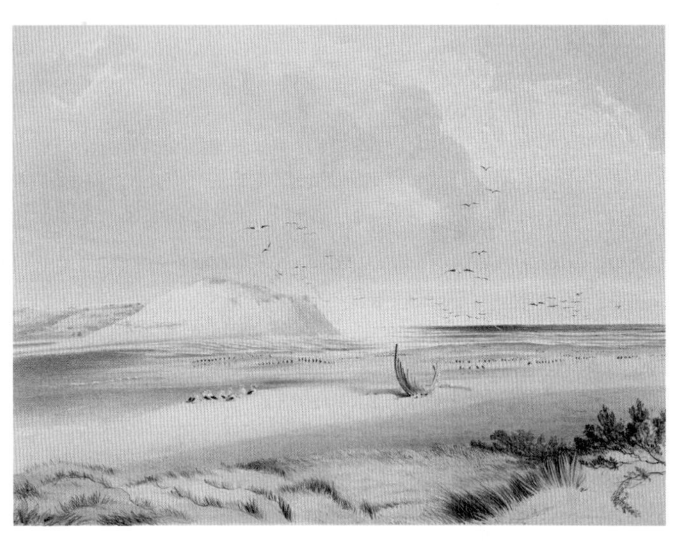

JAMES WILLIAM GILES
Scotland / Italy
born Aberdeen, Scotland, 1801
died Aberdeen, Scotland, 1870
after GEORGE FRENCH ANGAS
England / Australia
born Newcastle-upon-Tyne, England, 1822
died London, England, 1886
The sea mouth of the Murray
Ngarrindjeri country, South Australia
hand-coloured lithograph on paper
25.4 × 34.9 cm
South Australian Government Grant 1953
Art Gallery of South Australia, Adelaide
533G39

JAMES COLLINS HAWKER

Making a canoe 1901

from *Early Experiences in South Australia* 1901, E.S. Wigg & Son, Adelaide, Australia

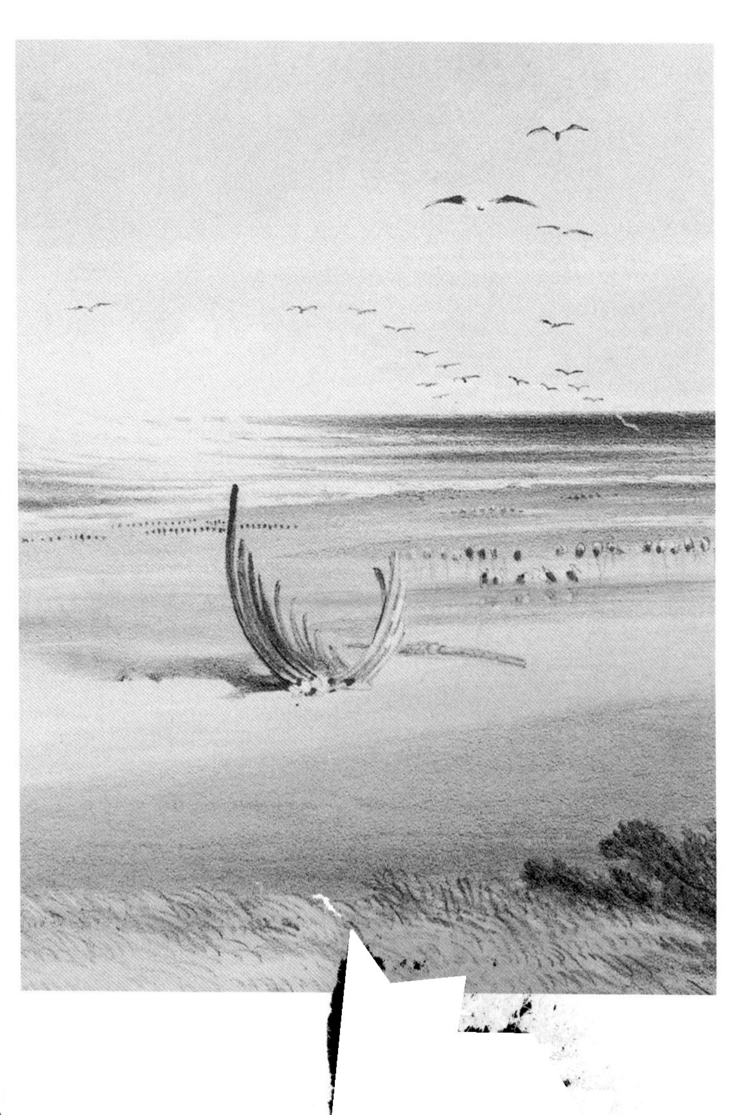

Postscript

This book has its origins in Jonathan Jones's project *untitled (Murray–Darling River hang)* 2012, presented as part of the 2012 Adelaide Biennial of Australian Art, *Parallel Collisions*, curated by Natasha Bullock and Alexie Glass at the Art Gallery of South Australia (AGSA).

This first iteration of the project was a work in three parts:

an installation in AGSA's Elder Wing of 42 colonial paintings, drawings and prints from the AGSA collection that depict the rivers, creeks and waterways of the Murray–Darling River system;

a set of exhibition benches referencing traditional Murray–Darling region canoes;

and, installed in the temporary exhibition galleries, a fallen river red gum sourced from the Murray–Darling region, illuminated and painted in white ochre. These three parts came together to challenge the western vision of landscape.

This artist's book is an attempt to iterate elements of Jones's project anew, and to develop further the project's relationship to the work of Tom Nicholson, whose project in the same biennial was installed in relation to Jones's, both in the Elder Wing and downstairs in the temporary exhibition galleries.

Each caption in this book has the following information, where known, presented in the following order: artist's name, nationality, birthplace and date, and place and date of death; artwork title and date; Aboriginal country; medium, dimensions, credit line, collection, and acquisition number. Measurements are in centimetres; height precedes width. (The exercise of connecting Aboriginal country with each image is based on limited information and as such is subject to inaccuracy. This information is not suitable for use in Native Title land claims. The spelling of each Aboriginal language group follows the most common usage.)

Acknowledgments

This project could not have been realised without the generous support, advice and leadership of many people, and Jonathan Jones gratefully acknowledges the following:

Uncle Lewis Yerloburka O'Brien for allowing this project to take place on his country; the knowledge, advice, stories and laughs of the Boggabilla aunties on the Macintyre River; Aunty Sandy Warren, Aunty Lorraine Tye, Uncle Stan Grant and Uncle Roy Kennedy on the Murrumbidgee; Uncle Badger Bates on the Darling; Aunty Lorraine Connelly-Northey on Billabong Creek; Uncle Moogy on the Coorong; and the late H.J. Wedge on the Lachlan River.

This project is dedicated to Aunty Yvonne Koolmatrie on the Murray, who through her tireless work is a constant reminder of the importance of the river system, and that nothing is lost. Our knowledge is in our country, in our elders and in our hearts.

This project owes much to Natasha Bullock and Alexie Glass, and to the support of the director Nick Mitzevich and staff at AGSA, in particular Nici Cumpston, who assisted in swimming against the institutional current, the installation team, who facilitated the hang of the Murray–Darling River works, and Tracey Dall, for preparing the images for this publication.

Thanks go to Luke Woodbridge and Chris Koolmatrie for their advice and for supplying the river red gum, and to Gene and Brian Sherman and the ongoing support of the Sherman Contemporary Art Foundation, Sydney.

The project would not have been possible without the boundless support of Genevieve O'Callaghan.

The project *untitled (Murray–Darling River hang)* was realised with the support of a New Work Grant from the Australia Council for the Arts.

This artist's book evolved from the insight and design skills of Žiga Testen, with the additional counsel of Brad Haylock.

This book would not have been possible without the friendship of Tom Nicholson.

Jonathan Jones
Murray–Darling views 2012–14
Edited by Brad Haylock

First edition 2014

Published by Surpllus Pty Ltd
PO Box 418
Flinders Lane 8009
Victoria, Australia
www.surpllus.com

Jonathan Jones is a Wiradjuri / Kamilaroi artist who lives in Sydney.

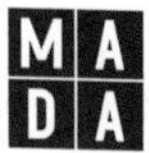

www.jonathanjones.com.au

Proofread by Genevieve O'Callaghan
Designed by Žiga Testen
Typeset in Adobe Caslon Pro
Printed by Brandenburgische Universitätsdruckerei Potsdam
ISBN 978-1-922099-09-9

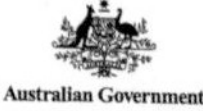

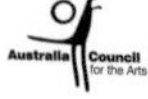

Cover image:
HENRY JAMES JOHNSTONE
England / Australia
born Birmingham, England, 1835
died London, England, 1907
Evening shadows, backwater of the Murray, South Australia 1880
unknown river country, south-east Australia
oil on canvas
120.6 × 184.1 cm
Gift of Mr Henry Yorke Sparks 1881
Art Gallery of South Australia, Adelaide
0.1

Cover image:
HENRY JAMES JOHNSTONE
England / Australia
born Birmingham, England, 1835
died London, England, 1907
Evening shadows, backwater of the Murray, South Australia 1880
south-east Australia
oil on canvas
120.6 x 184.1 cm
Gift of Mr Henry Yorke Sparks 1881
Art Gallery of South Australia, Adelaide
0.1

Tom Nicholson
Evening shadows

Surpllus

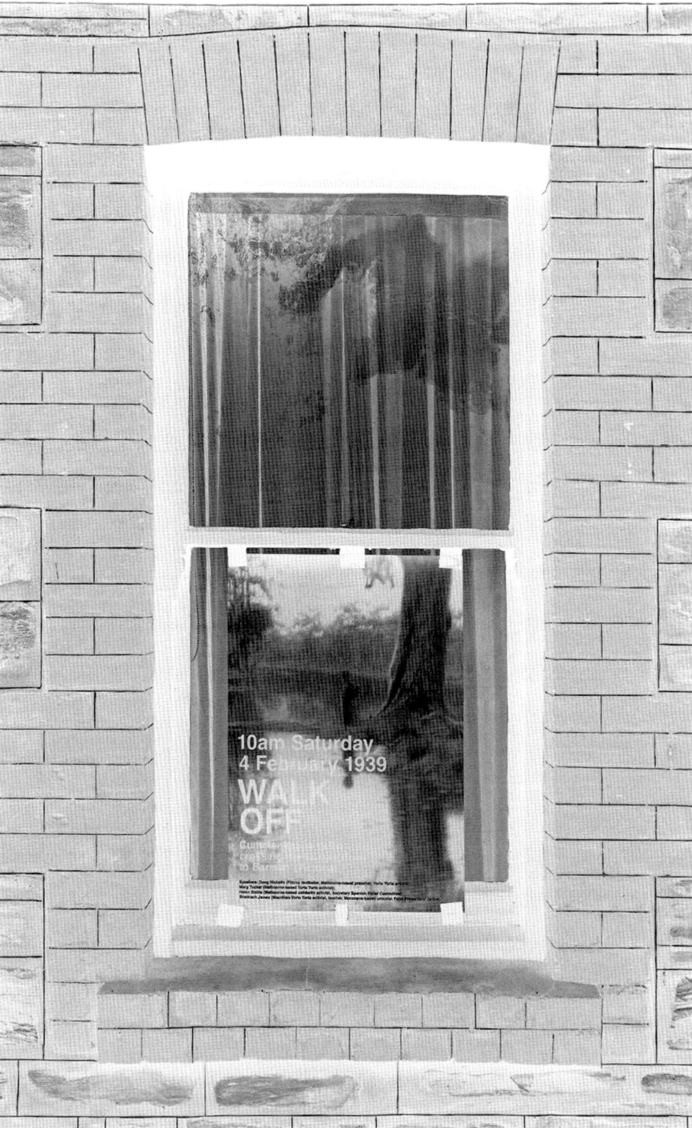
10am Saturday

"I am very proud to be able to stand here today and talk to people who belong to the Yorta Yorta tribe, to people who come from Cummeragunja. Cummeragunja's got a great meaning for many people. There are thousands of descendants from this place, and everybody maintains their strong link with the land. The Walk Off we're commemorating today was a very special event. It wasn't an easy thing for people to leave their only home, the only home they knew, land that belonged to us, and the only remnant of the land we had left. It was an act of courage. It was an act of political defiance. It was

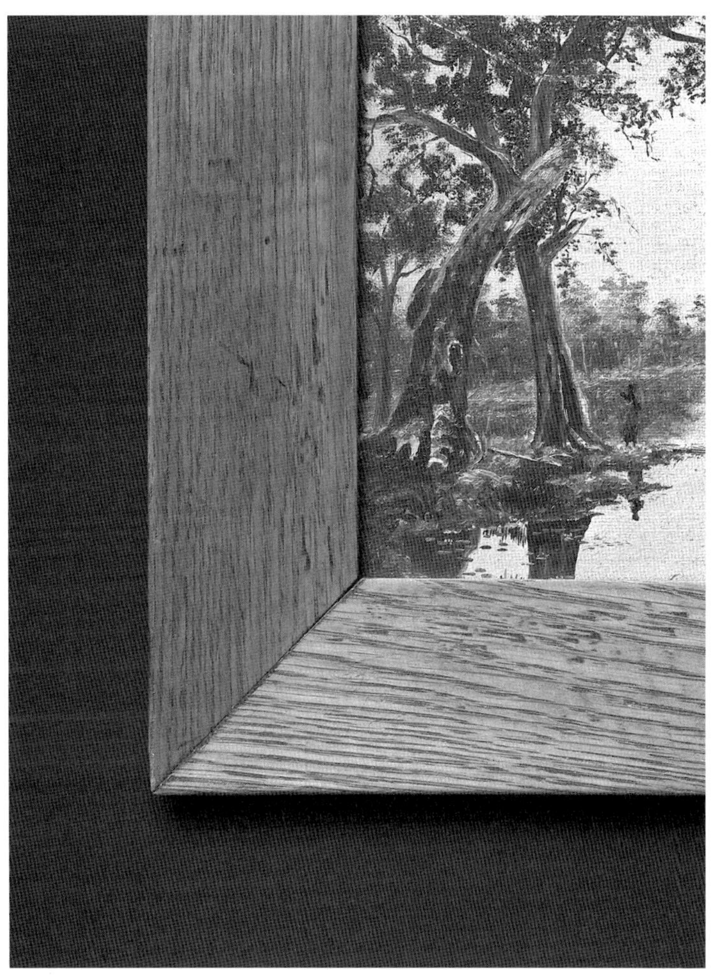

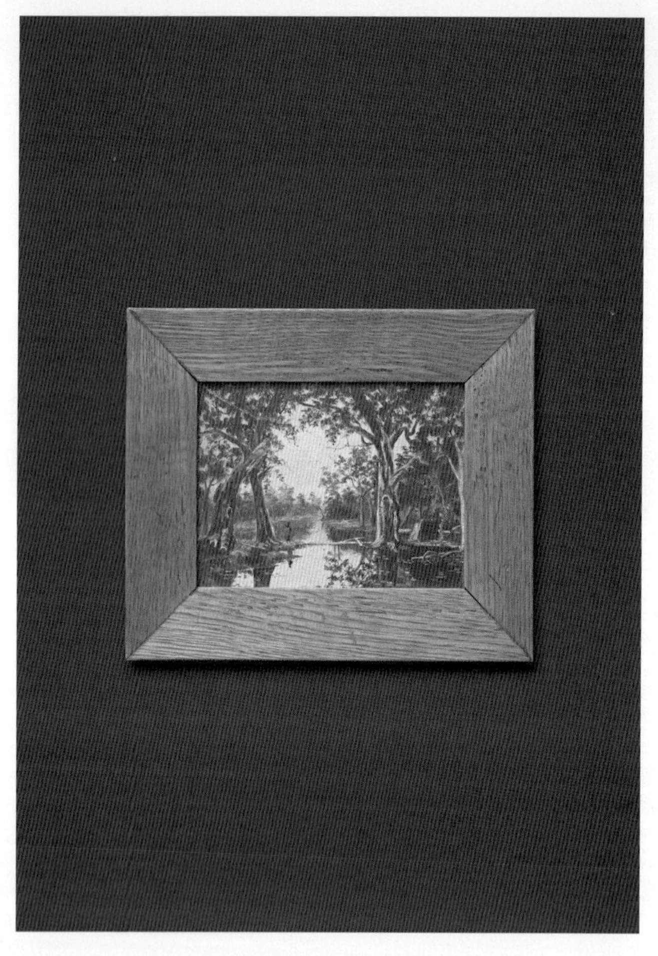

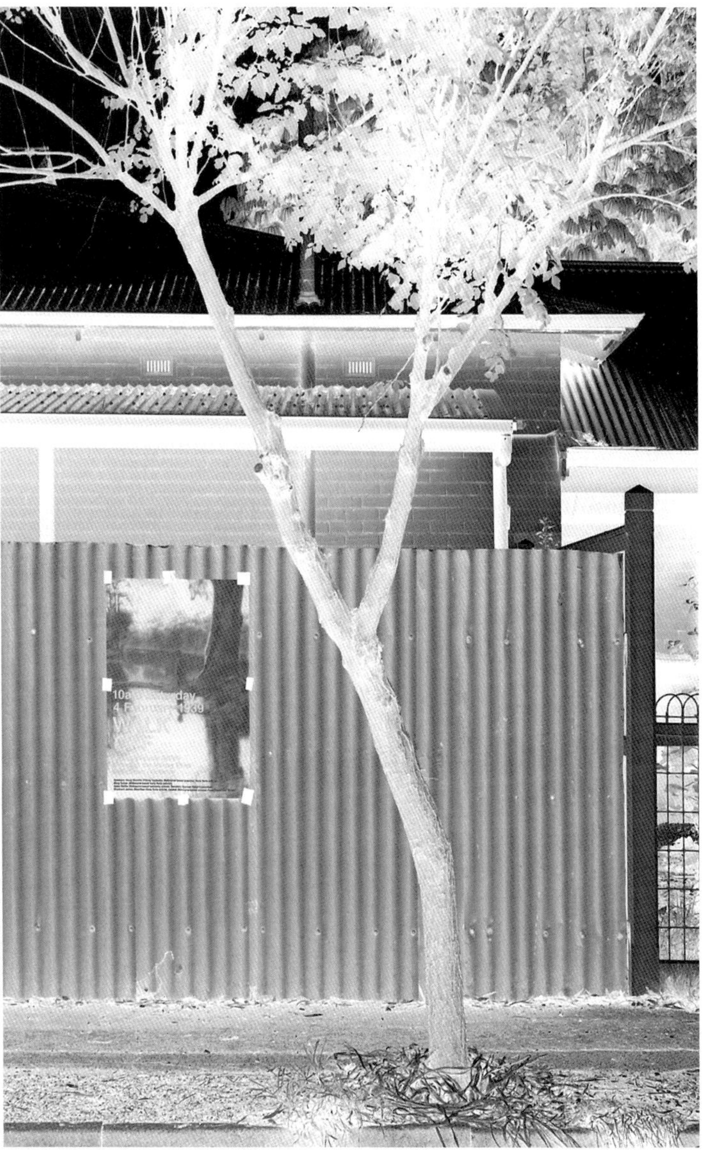

an act of self-determination. It was taking control of our own affairs and moving where we wanted to go, away from that control that the government had over us. It wasn't easy. It was hardship. And today, in us marching, what we're doing at Cummeragunja today, and what everybody, everyone of you here supporting Cummeragunja, as your home and the place where we all come from, it's a very important thing.

"What we're doing at Cummeragunja is walking. When I say 'walking' I mean we're going under our own steam. We're standing on our feet, not our knees. We're going ahead. We're refusing to be controlled."

Henry James Johnstone's *Evening shadows, backwater of the Murray, South Australia* 1880,

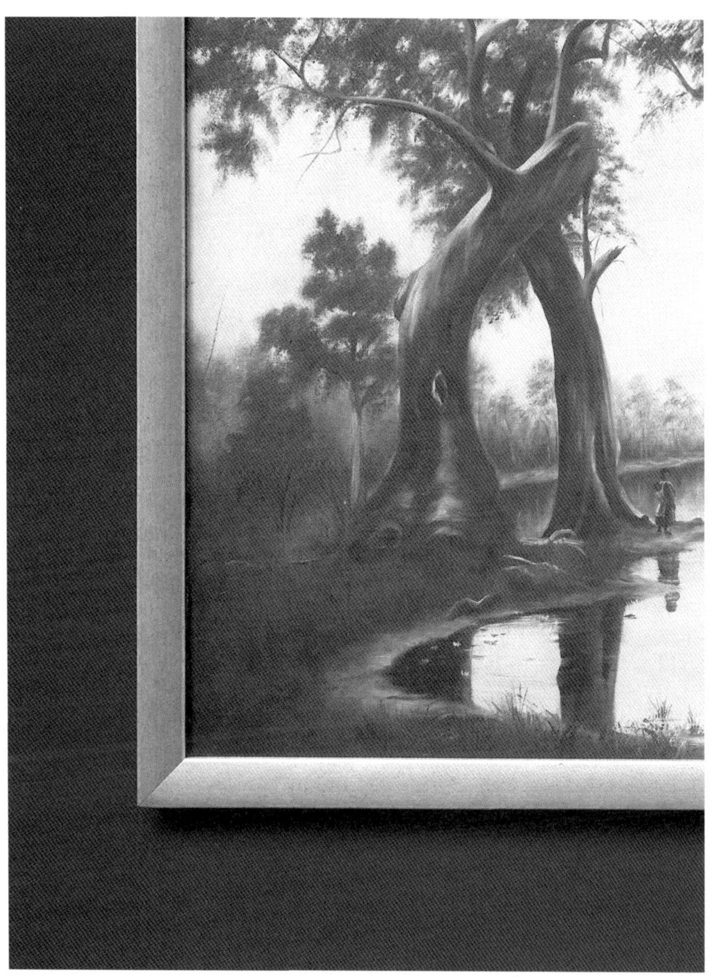

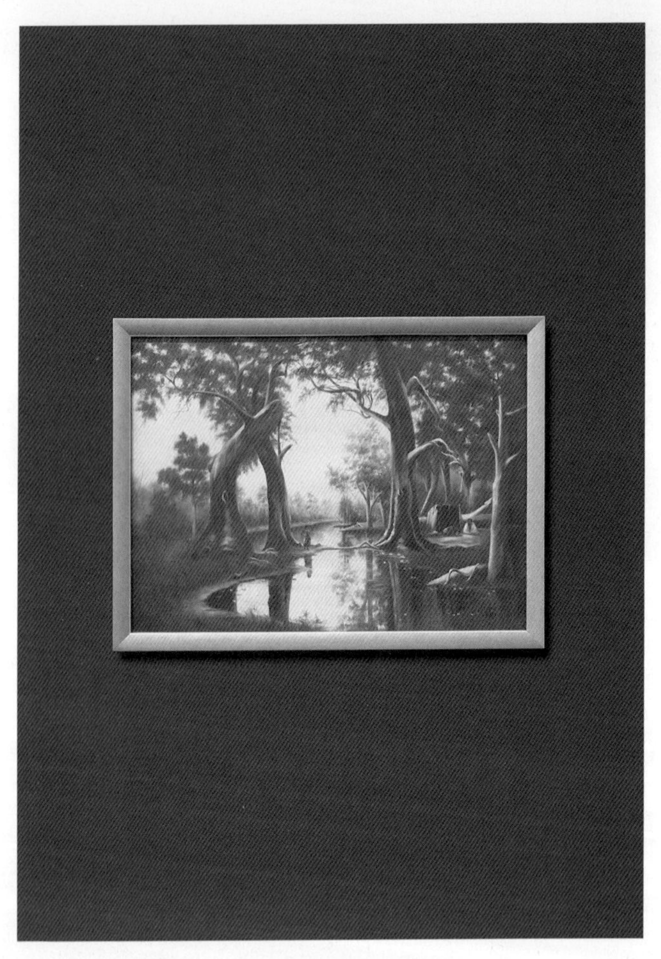

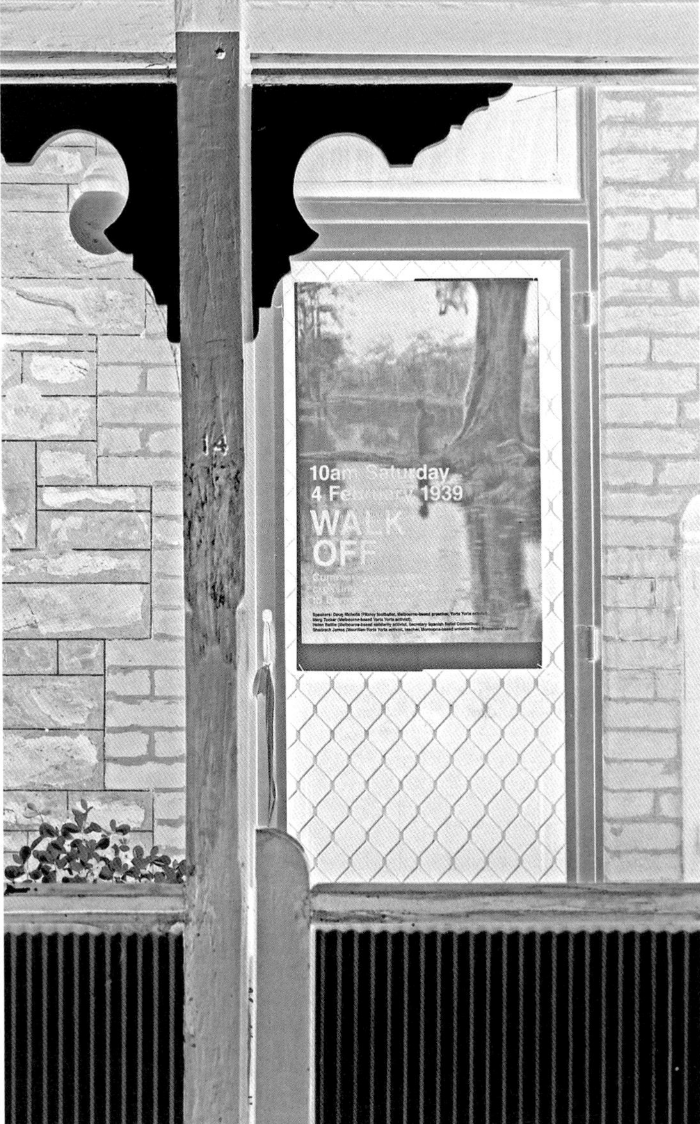
14
10am Saturday
4 February 1939
WALK
OFF

It is 24 November 1988 when the young Yorta Yorta lawyer and activist Sandra Bailey speaks these words to a crowd of Yorta Yorta people, who gather on the banks of the Murray River at Barmah before they march across the river to Cummeragunja,

held in the Art Gallery of South Australia in Adelaide, is the most celebrated of several versions he paints of the same scene,

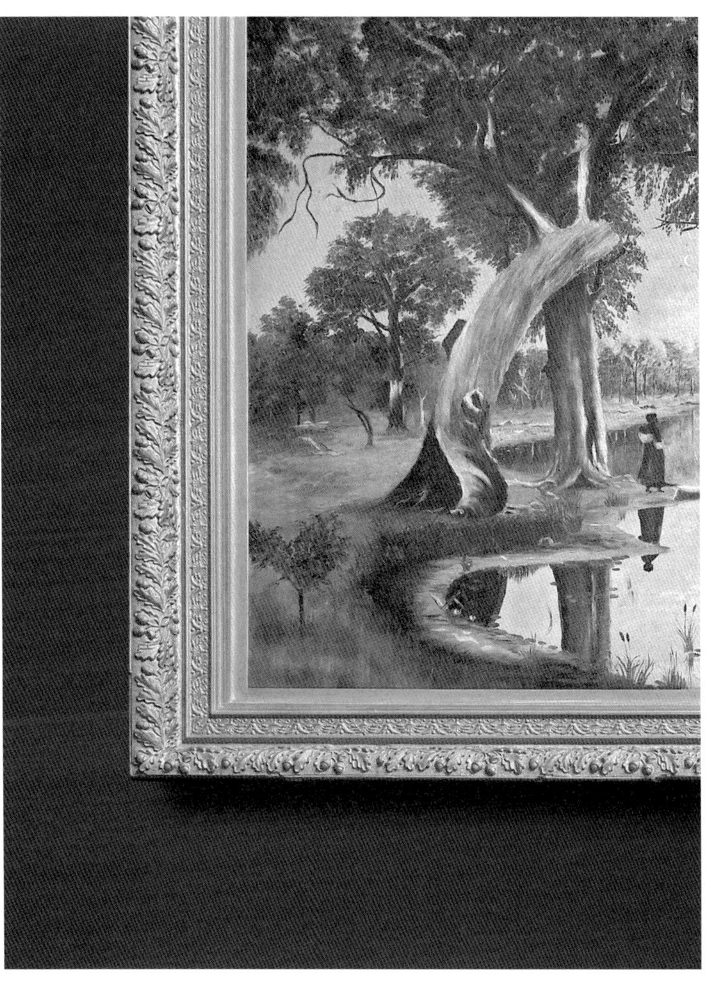

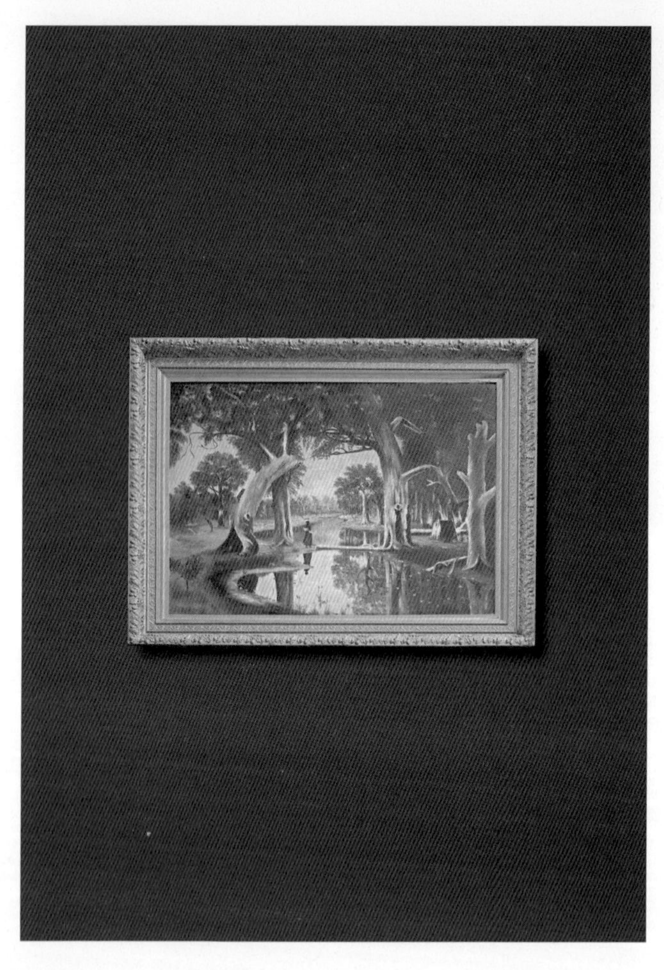

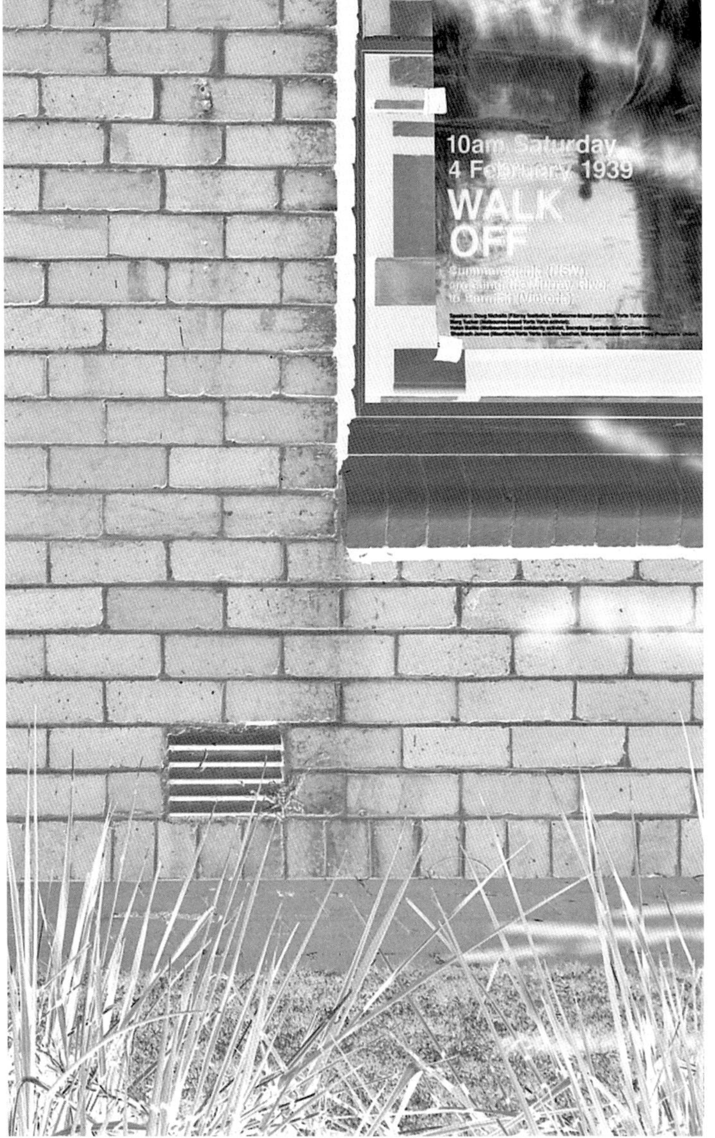
10am Saturday
4 February 1939
WALK
OFF

an event filmed by Uncle Wayne Atkinson, Yorta Yorta elder and founder of the Koori Oral History Program at the State Library of Victoria in 1987.

an Aboriginal woman with a child on her back crossing the Murray River at dusk,

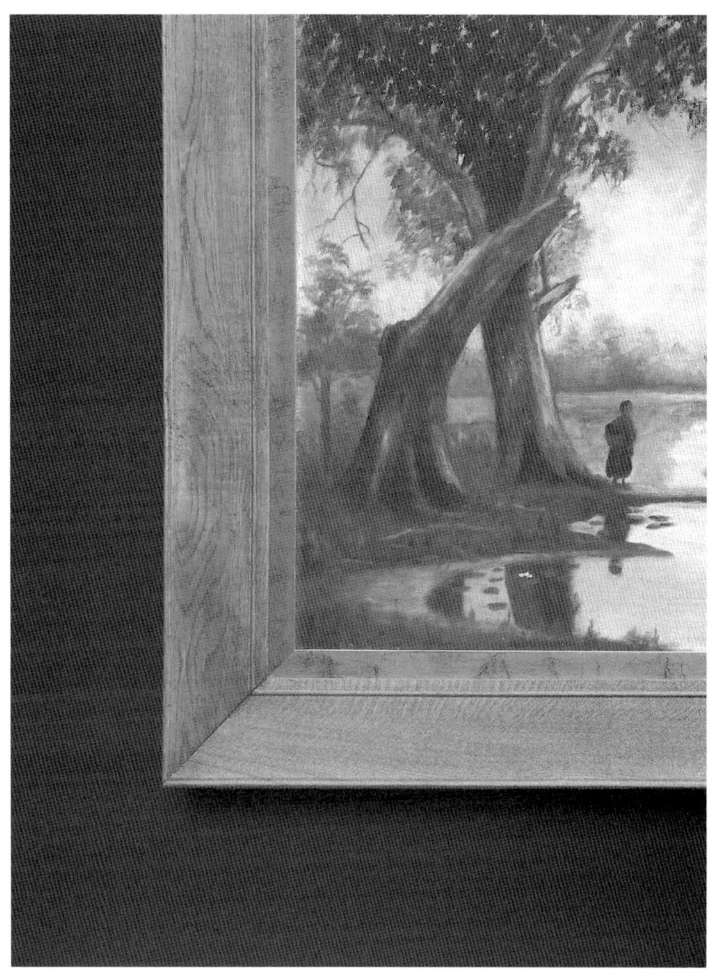

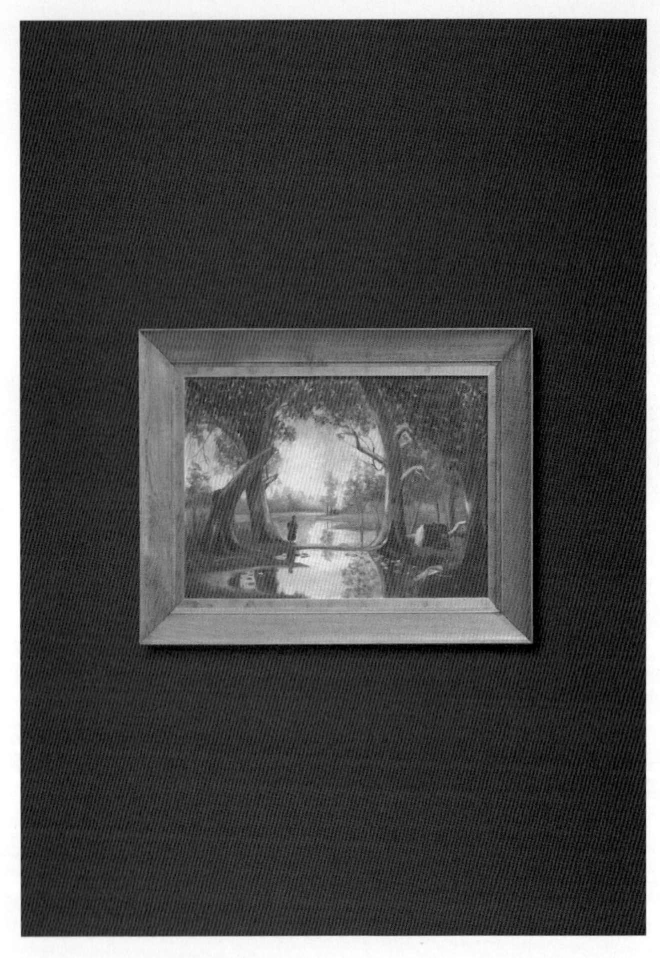

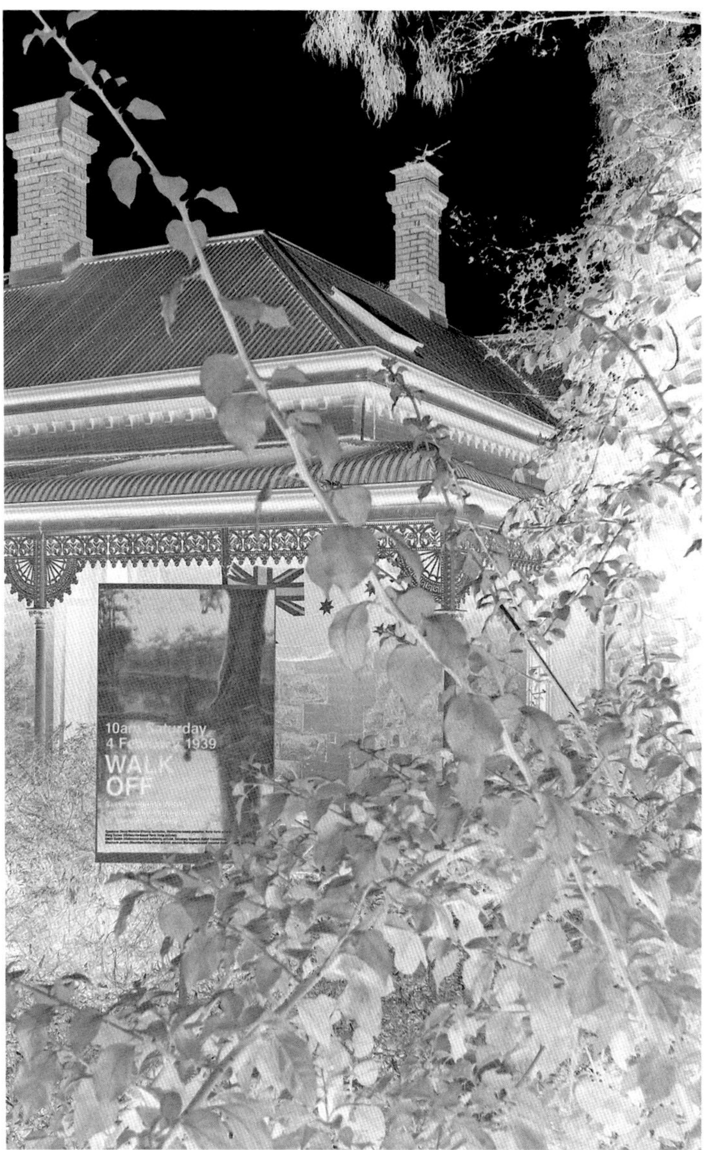
WALK
OFF

Atkinson's footage captures Yorta Yorta people celebrating 100 years since the establishment of Cummeragunja in 1888, when Yorta Yorta people choose a site on the New South Wales side of the Murray River, and name that site "Cummeragunja", "my home", where they establish a thriving community.

an image marked by its crisp realism

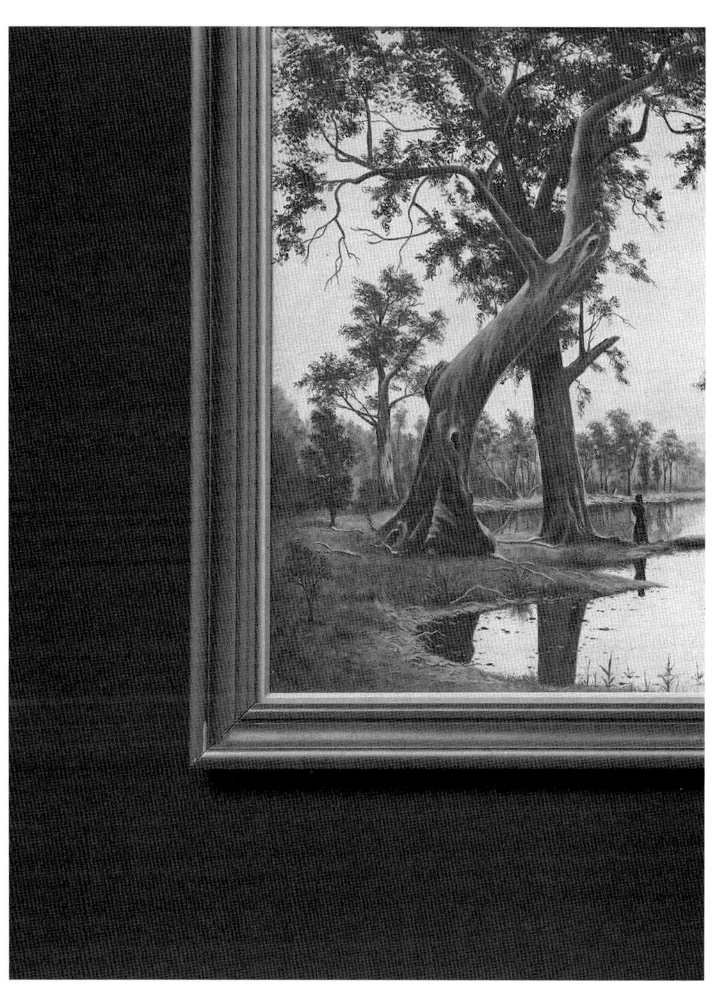

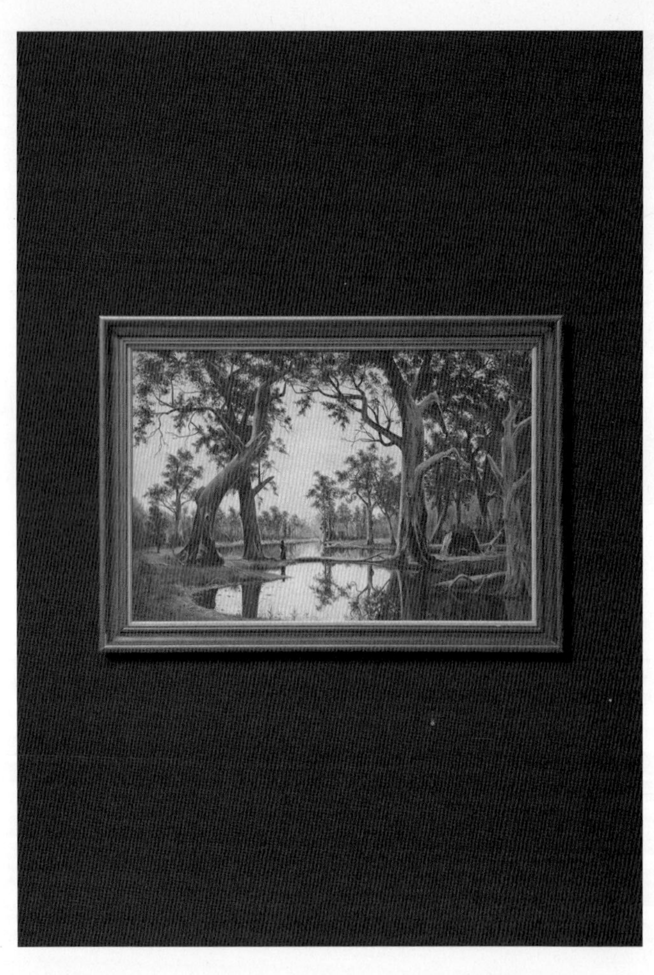

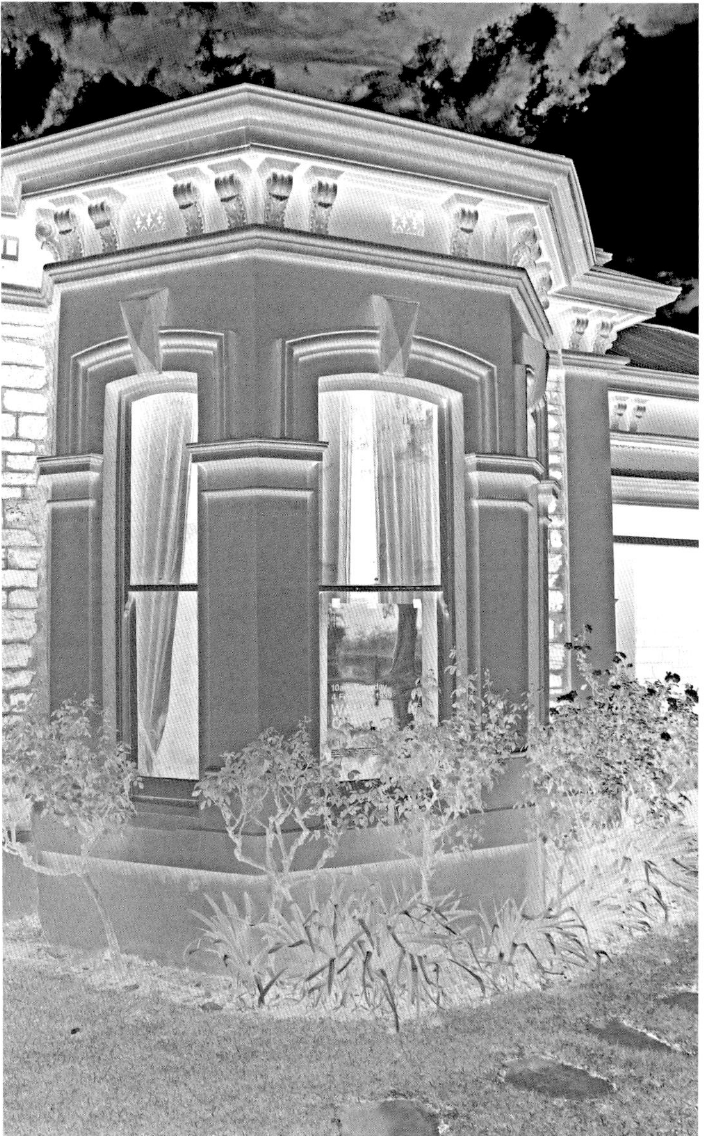

Atkinson's footage also captures Yorta Yorta people commemorating the "Walk Off",

and by its (classically nineteenth-century) allegory of fading light.

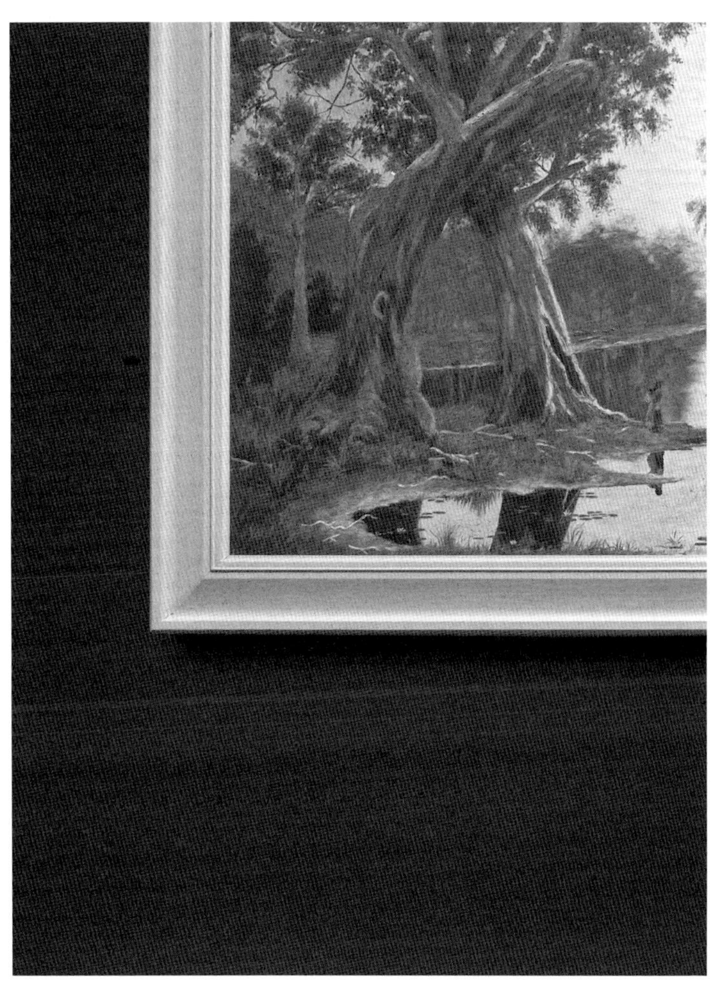

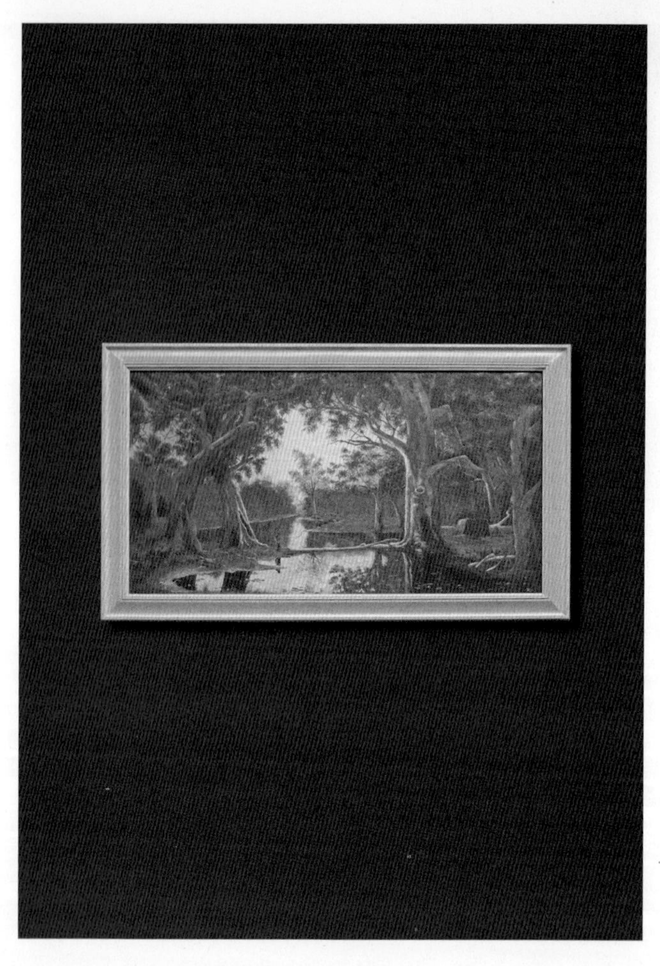

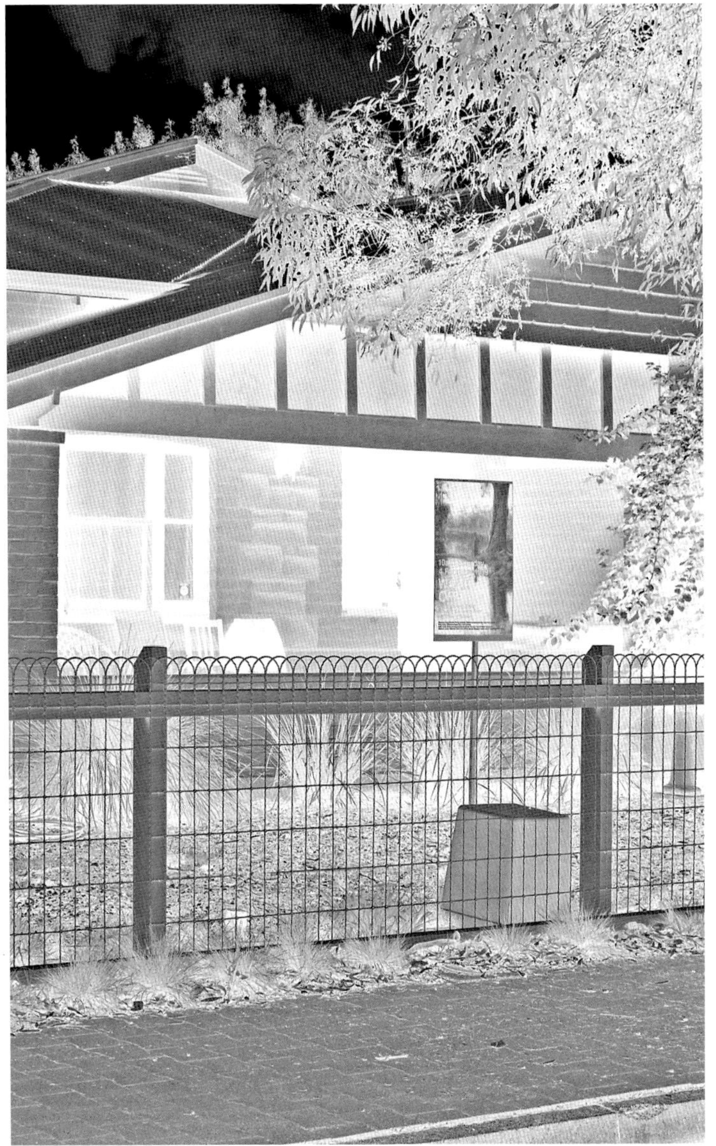

4 February 1939,

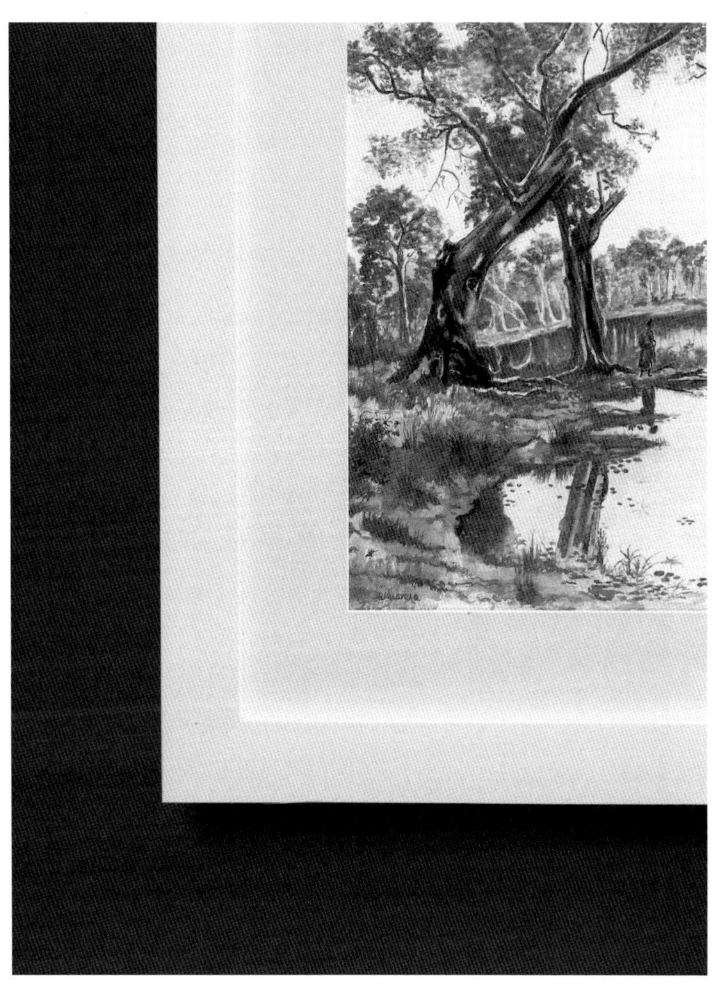

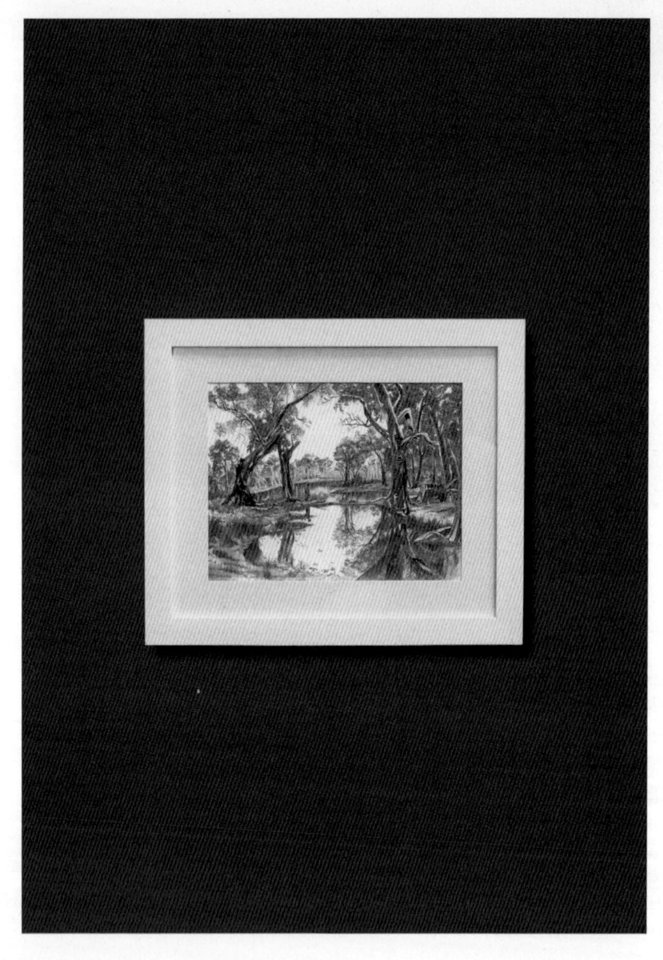

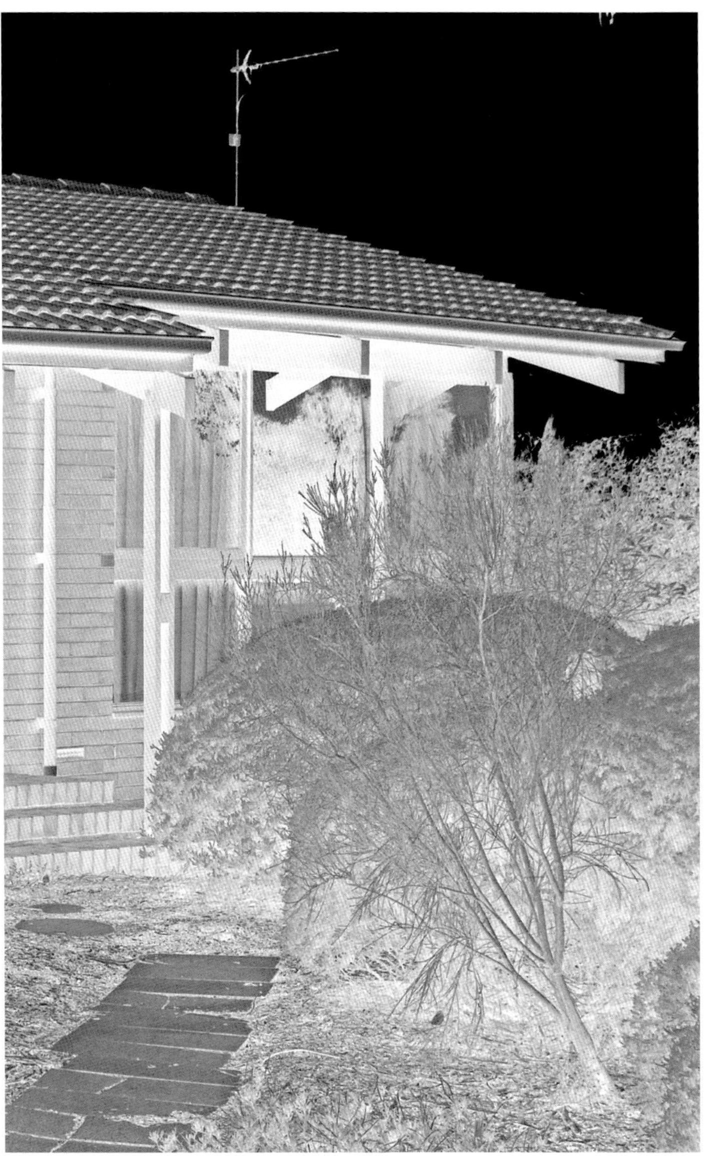

when Yorta Yorta people cross the Murray River and set up camp on the Victorian side of the river at Barmah in protest against the extreme levels of control and deprivation that increasingly mark the oppressive conditions at Cummeragunja.

Starting his career as a commercial photographer and initially working in his father's studio,

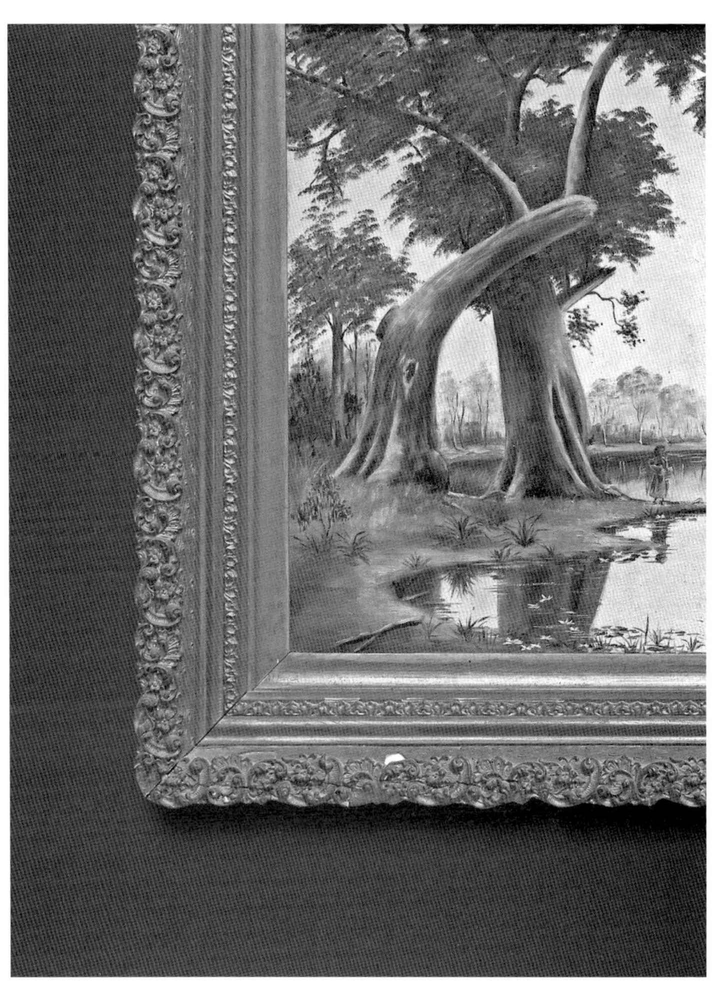

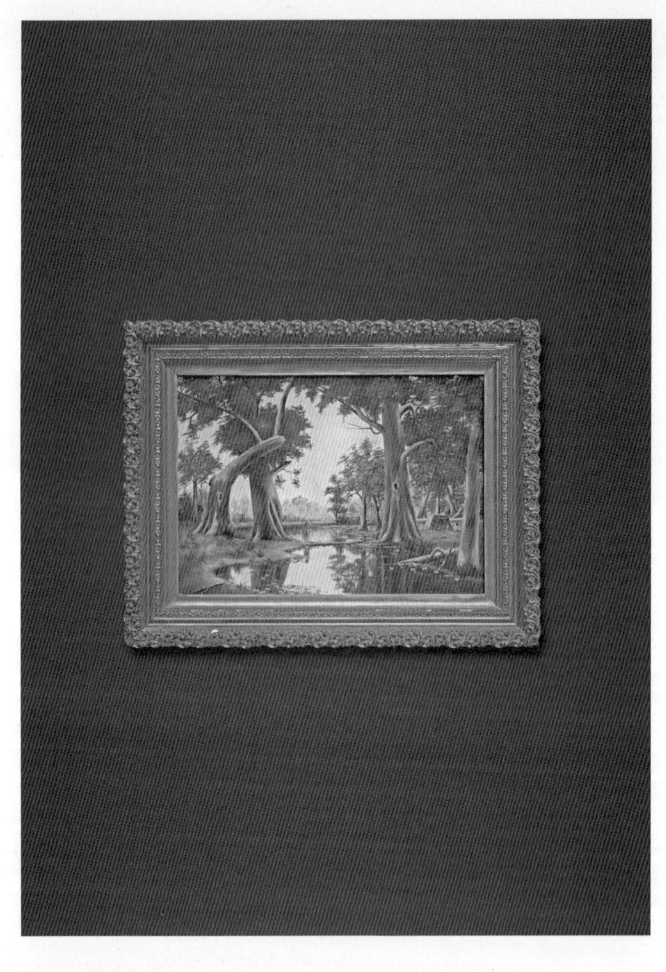

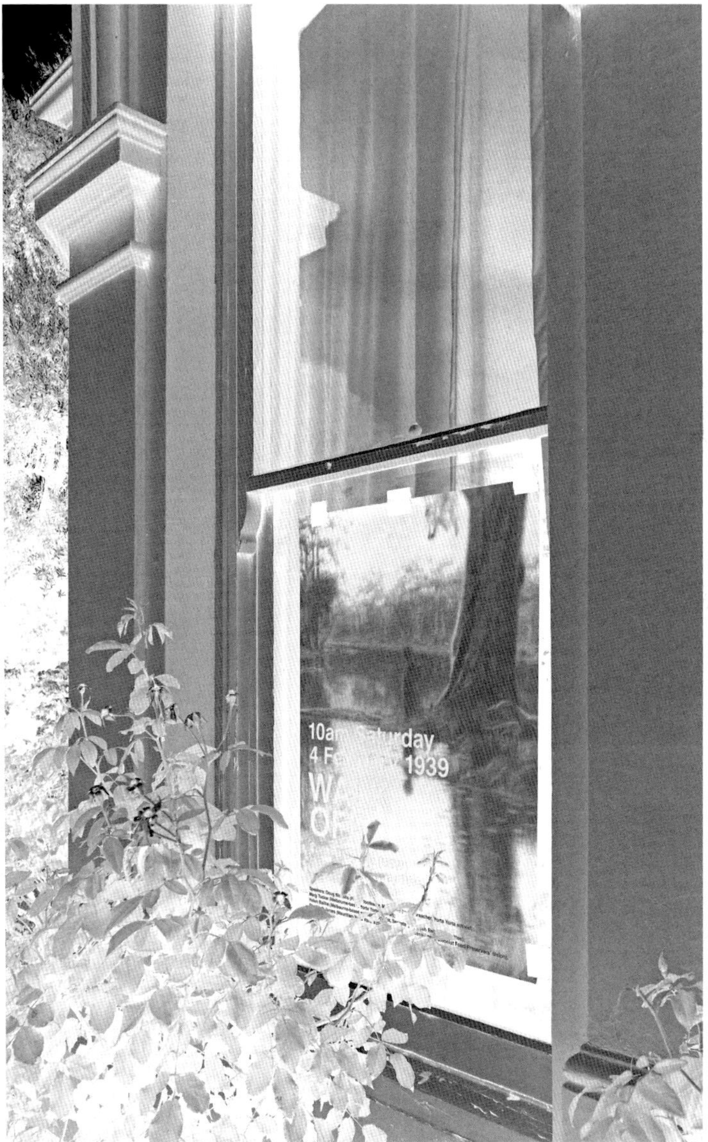
1939

In Atkinson's footage we see a range of speakers from different generations of the Yorta Yorta diaspora, including the young Aboriginal rights activist Monica Morgan, the CEO of the Redfern Aboriginal Medical Service, Naomi Mayers, and elders Aunty Merle Jackomos and Aunty Elizabeth Morgan-Hoffman.

later establishing one of Melbourne's most fashionable photographic studios in the 1860s,

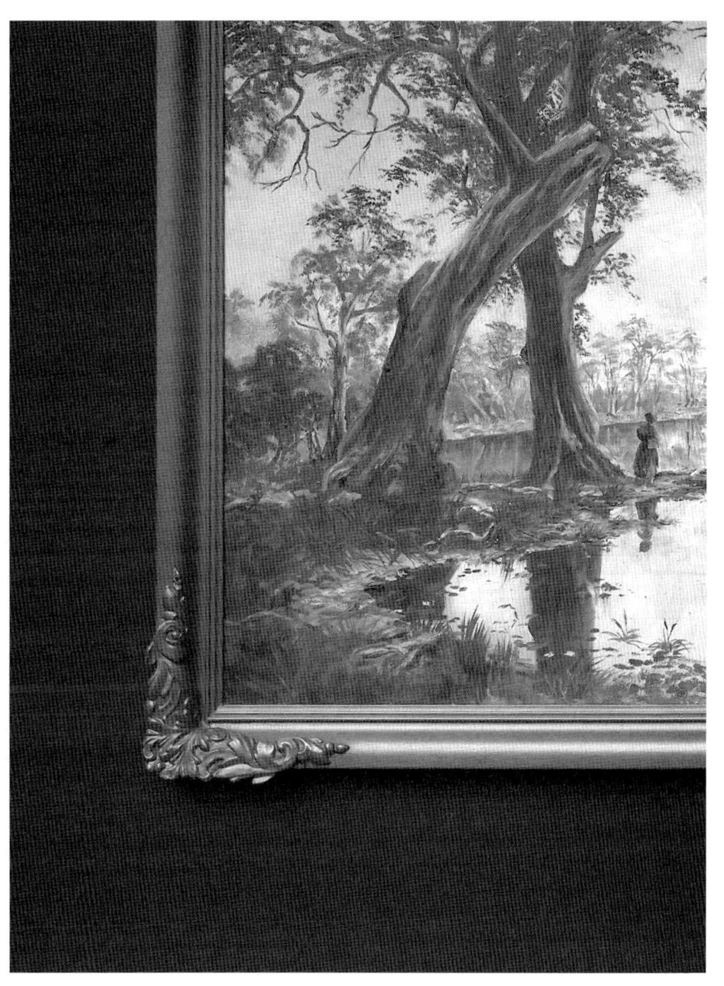

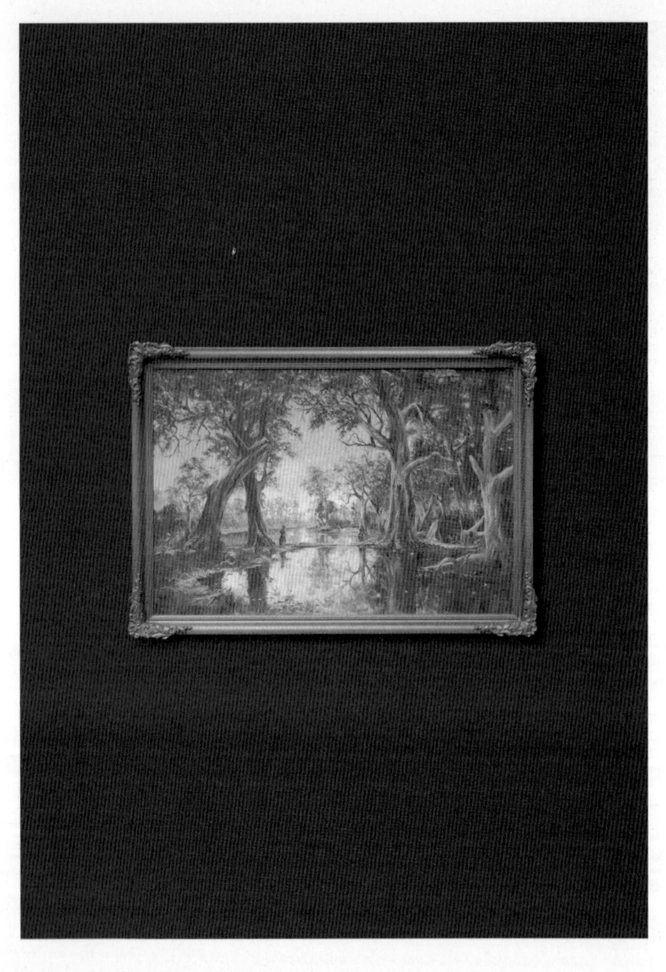

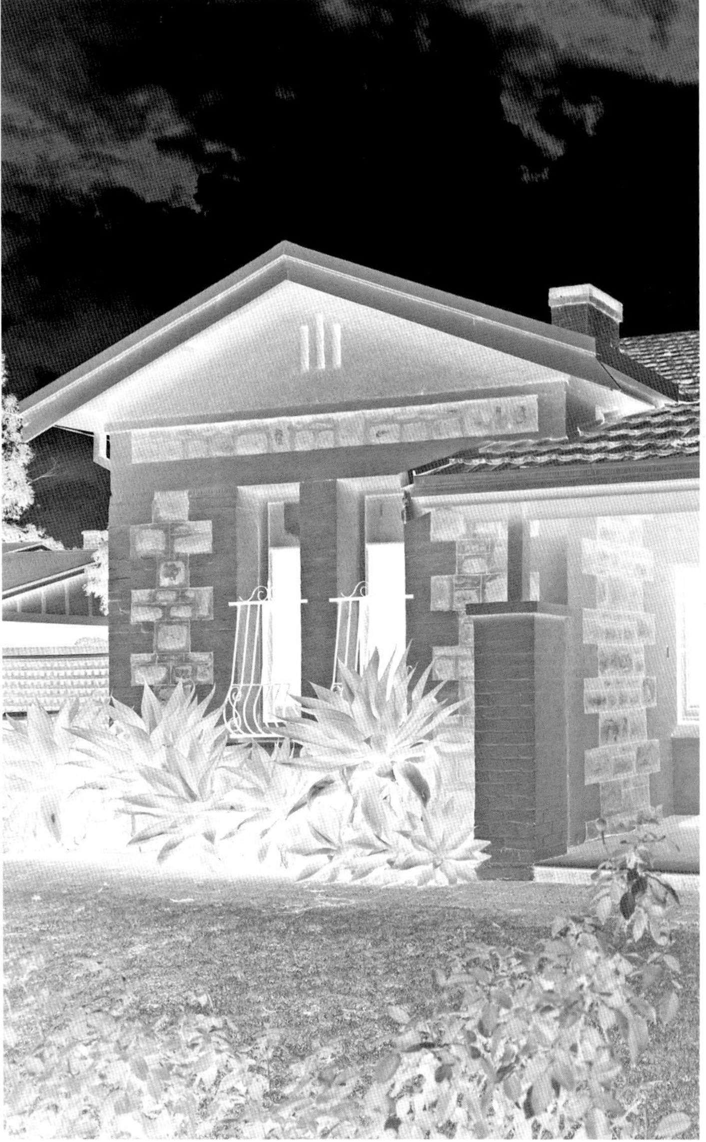

They describe the gestation of the Walk Off and the importance of early pan-Aboriginal leaders like the Yorta Yorta activists Jack Patten and William Cooper,

Johnstone, O'Shannessy & Co.,

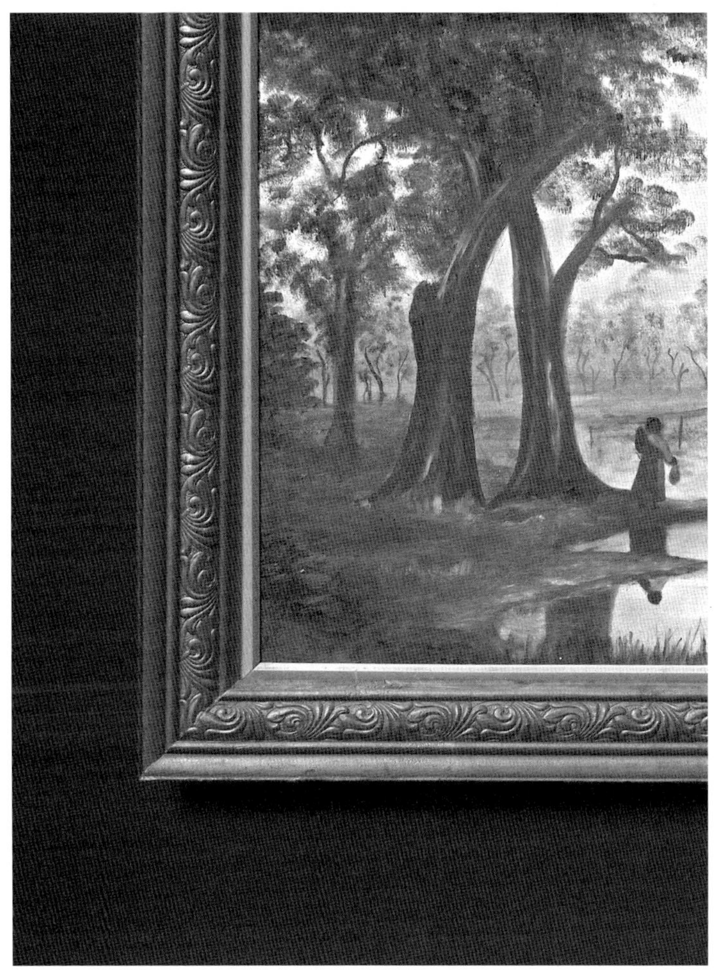

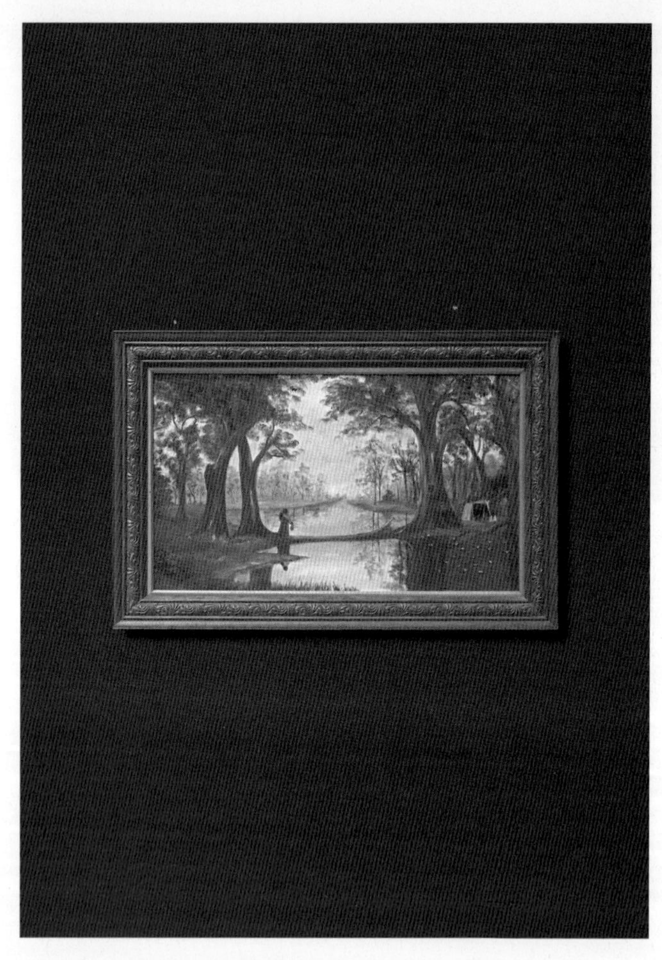

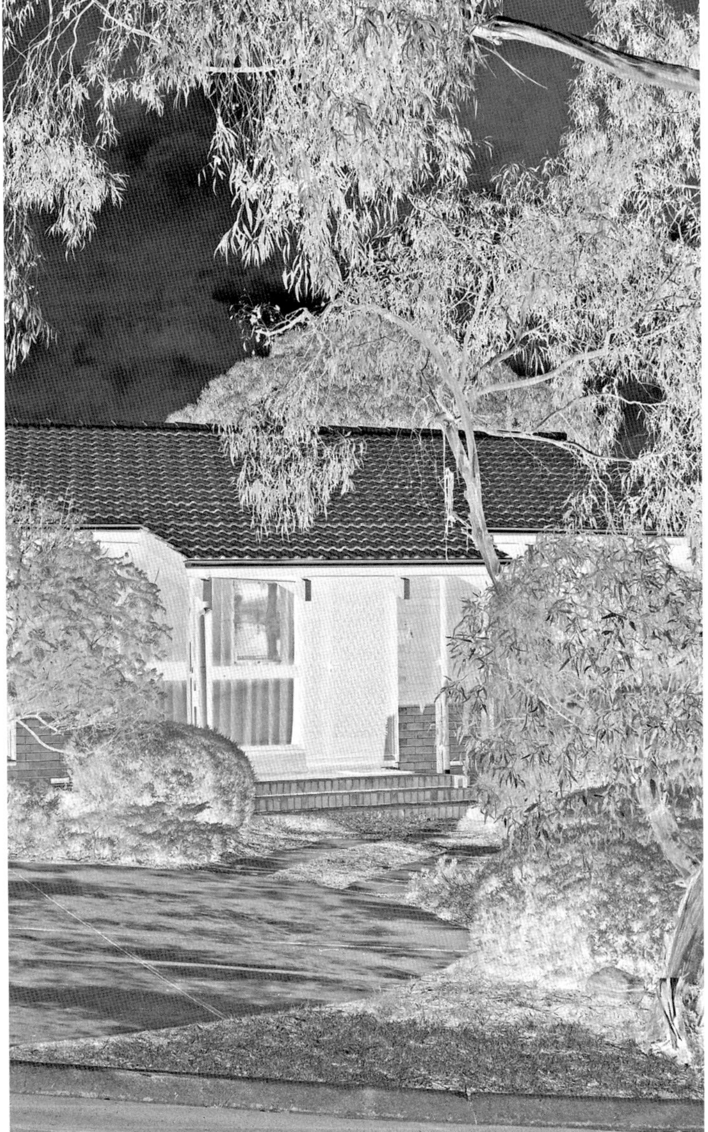

as well as the Fitzroy footballer, preacher and
Yorta Yorta man Doug Nicholls,

Johnstone trains as a painter,

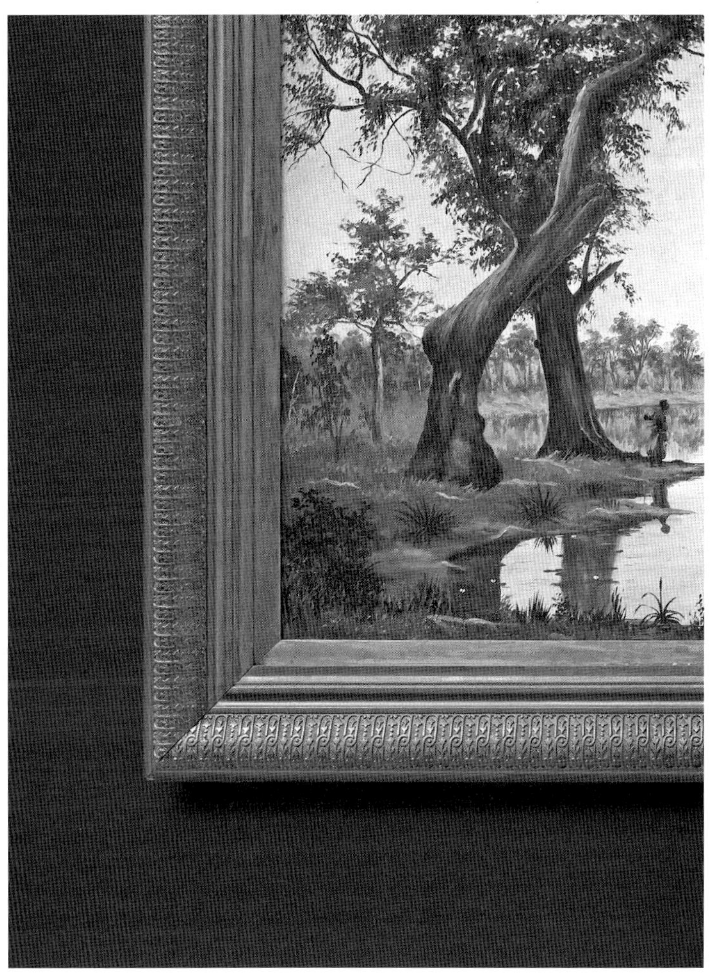

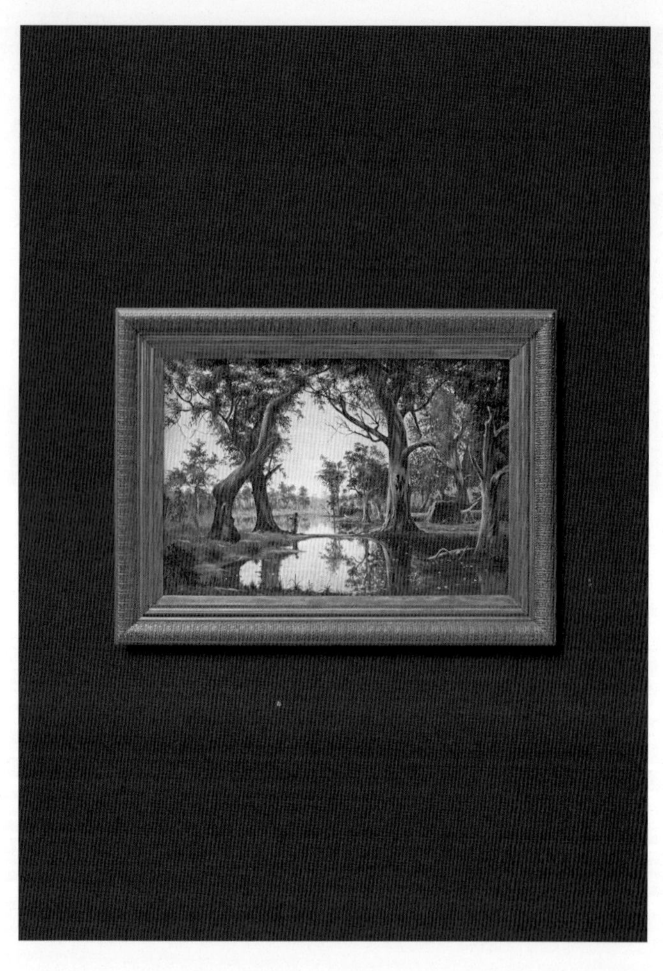

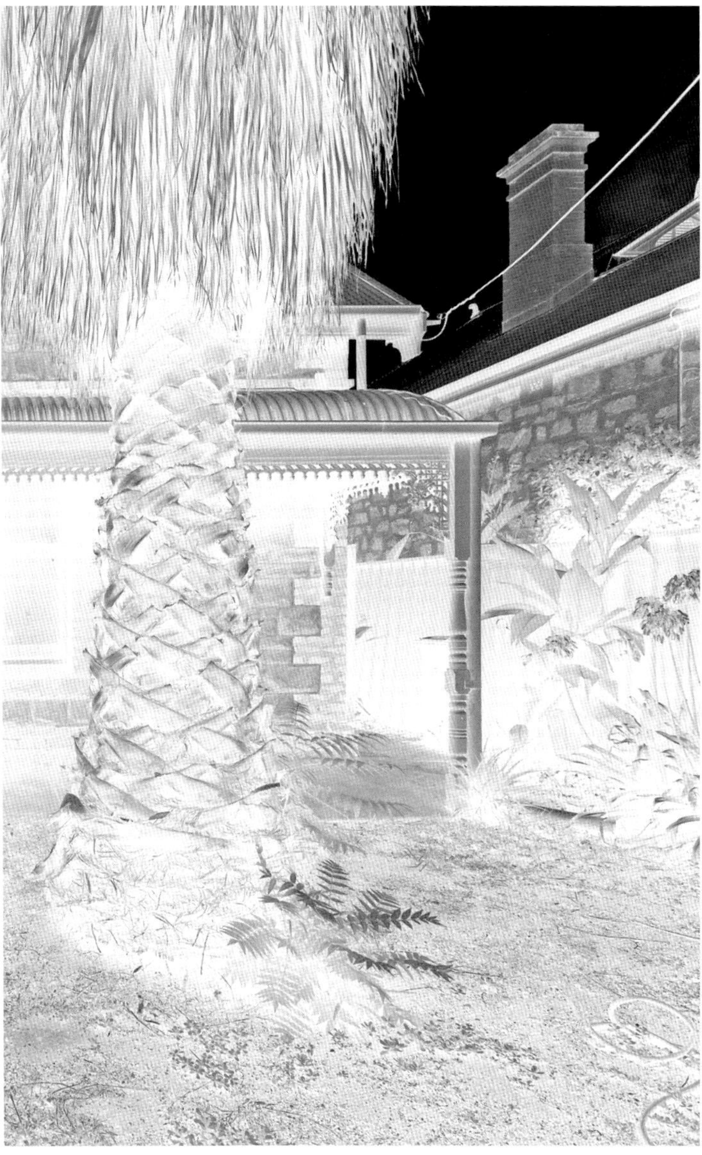

the Melbourne-based Yorta Yorta activist
Marg Tucker,

but never loses the vestiges of his origins in photography,

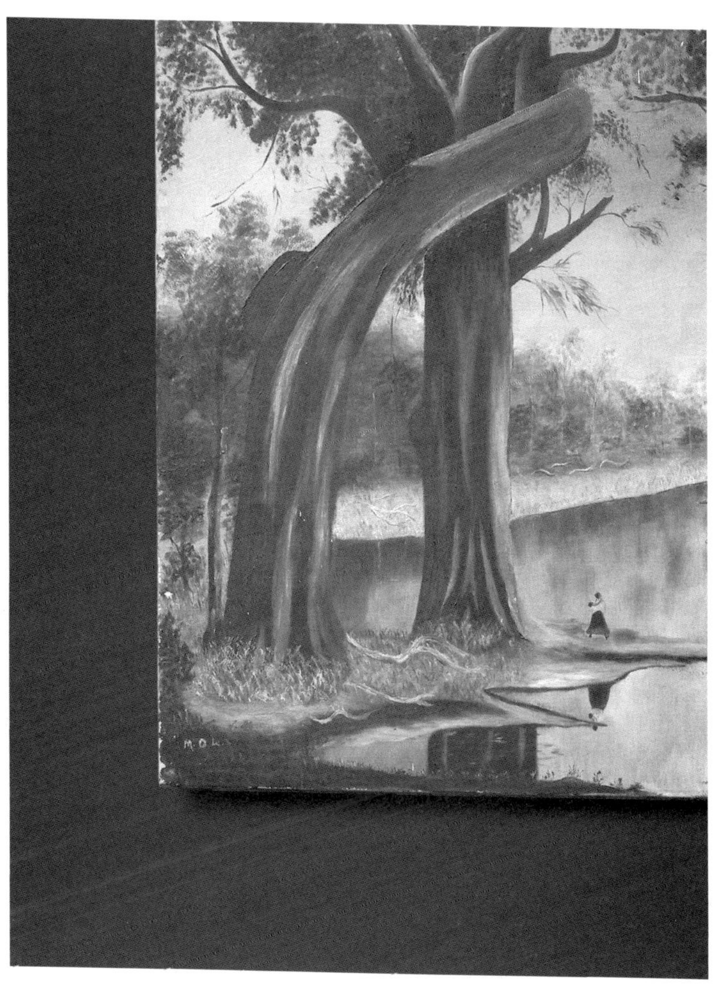

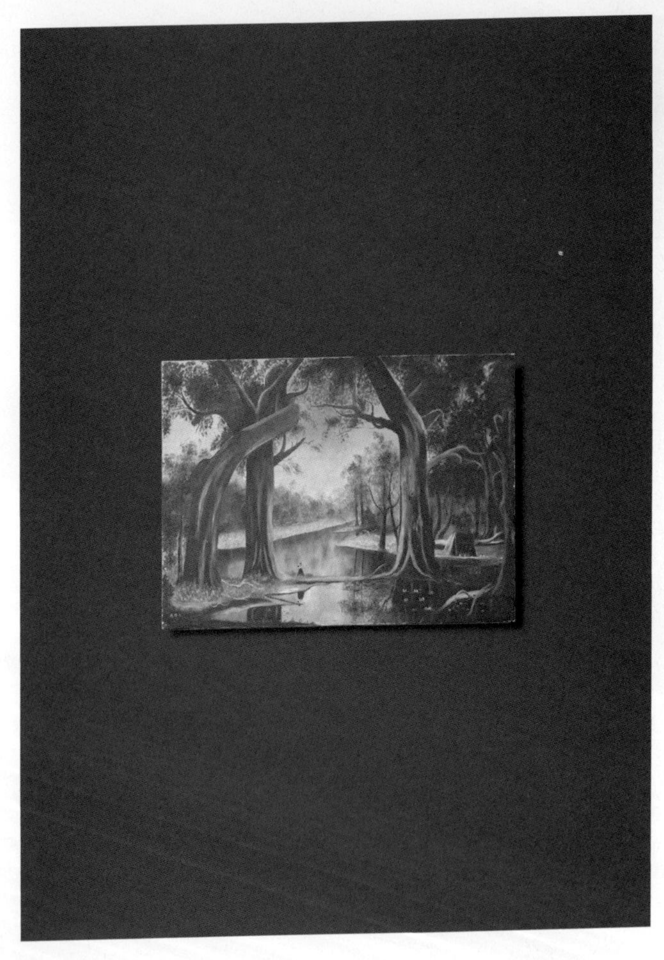

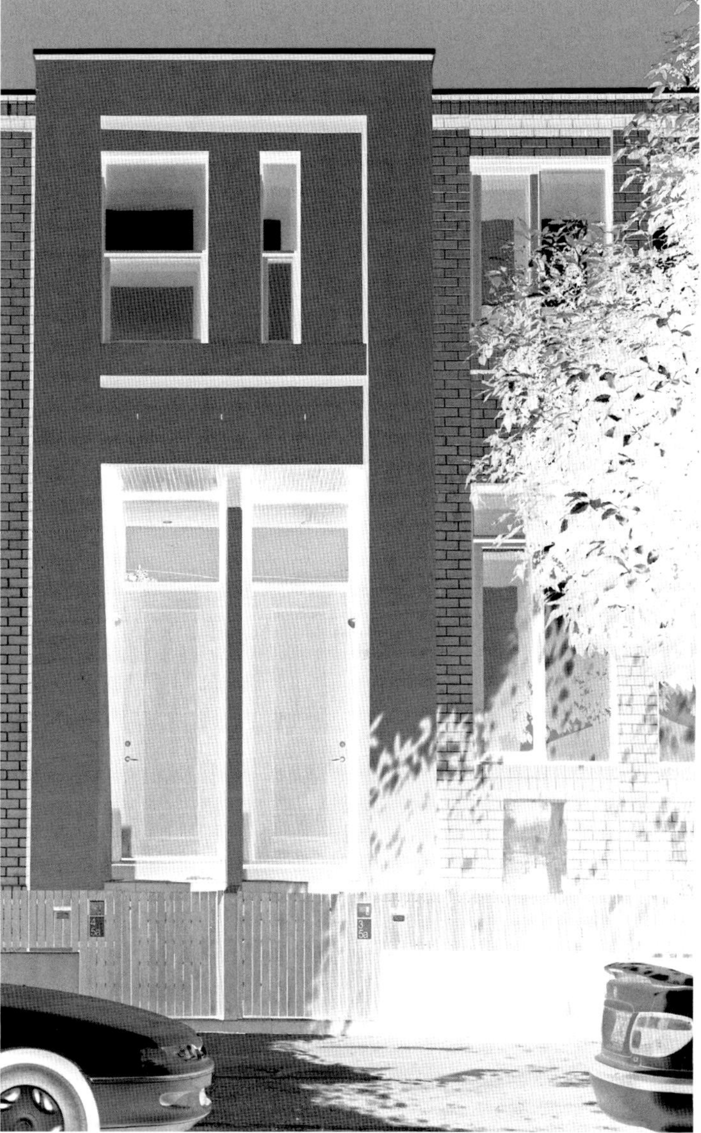

Helen Bailie, a non-Aboriginal supporter at the same time also working in solidarity with the fight against European fascism as Secretary of the Spanish Relief Committee,

evident in the pictorial organisation of *Evening shadows* and its all-over attention to the details of the landscape,

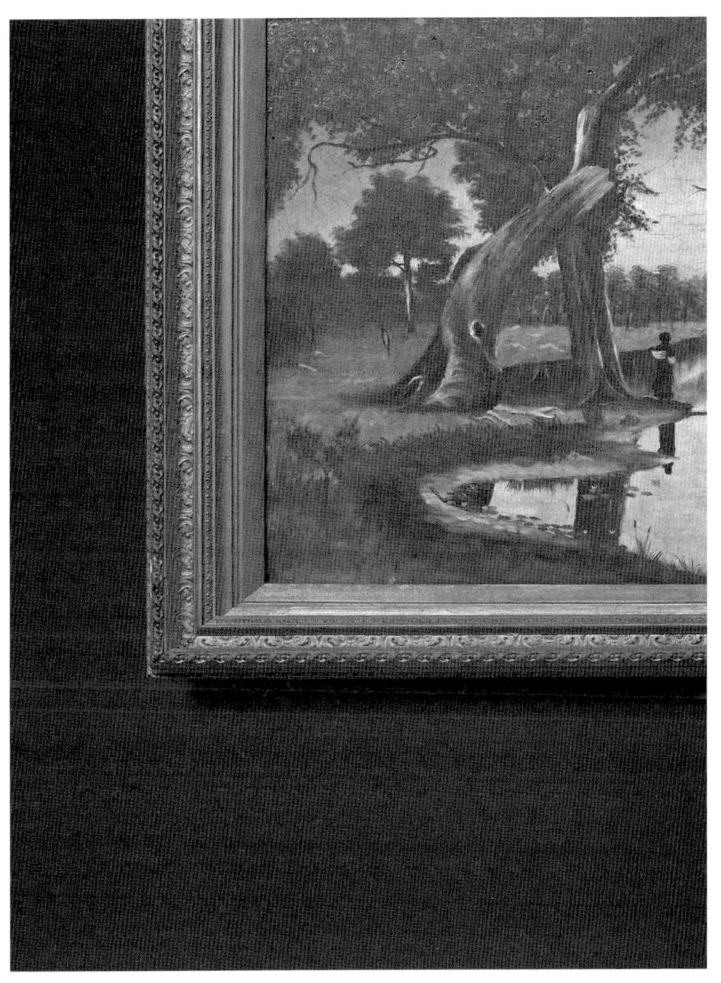

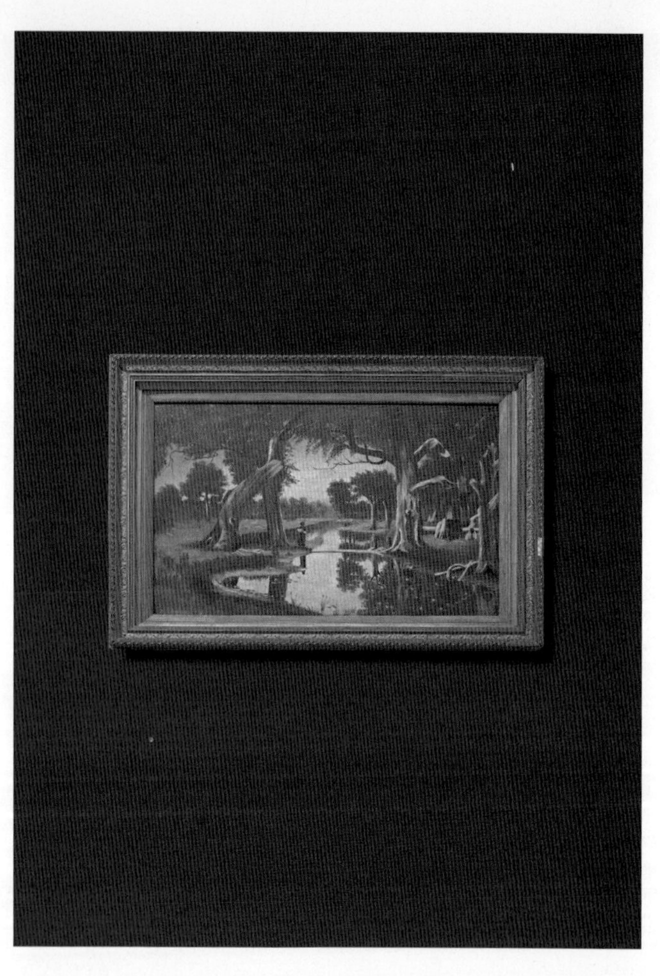

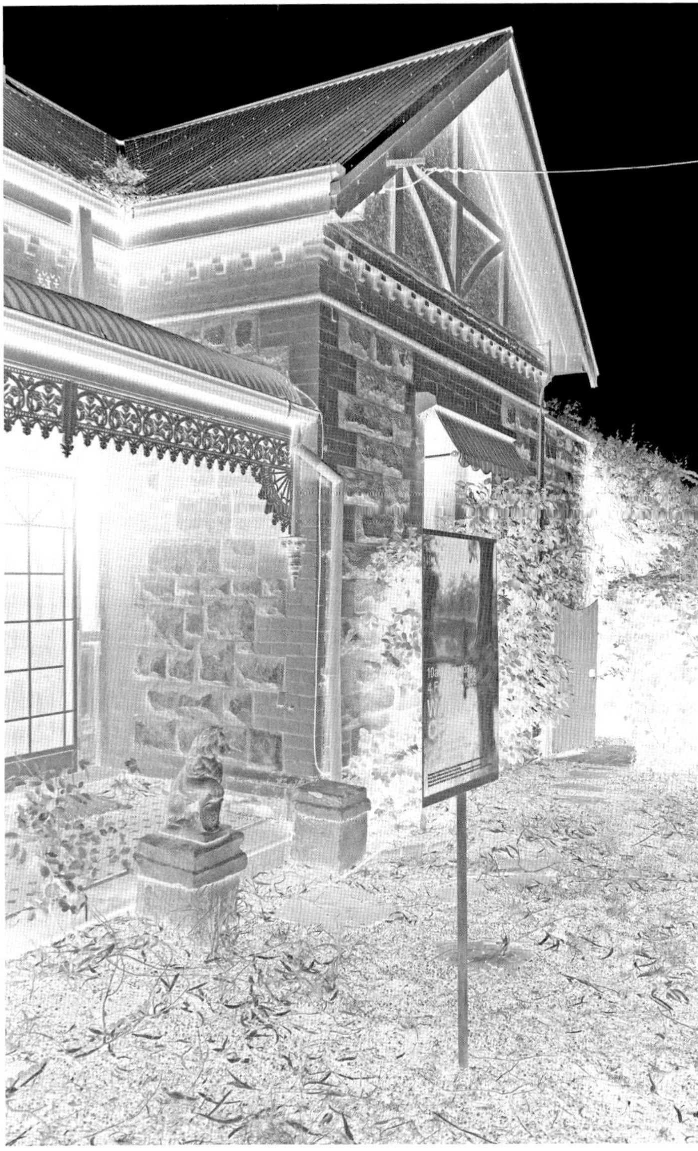

and Shadrach James, the Yorta Yorta trade unionist whose Mauritian father, Thomas James, is a significant figure and educator in the early history of Cummeragunja.

but also in the painting's proliferation as a photographic edition that Johnstone himself publishes,

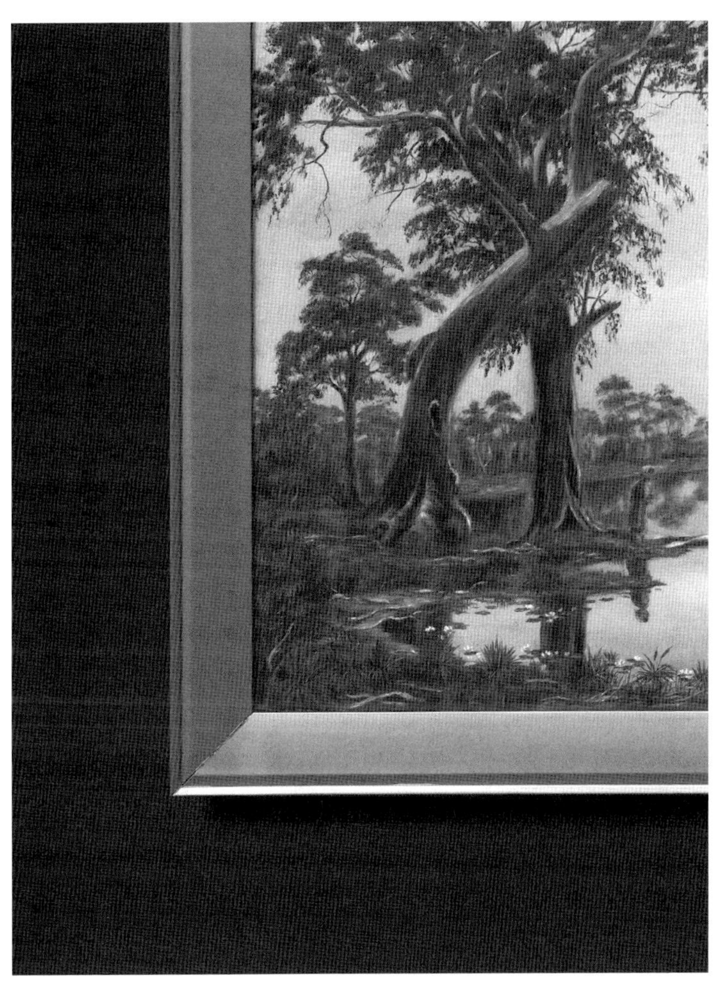

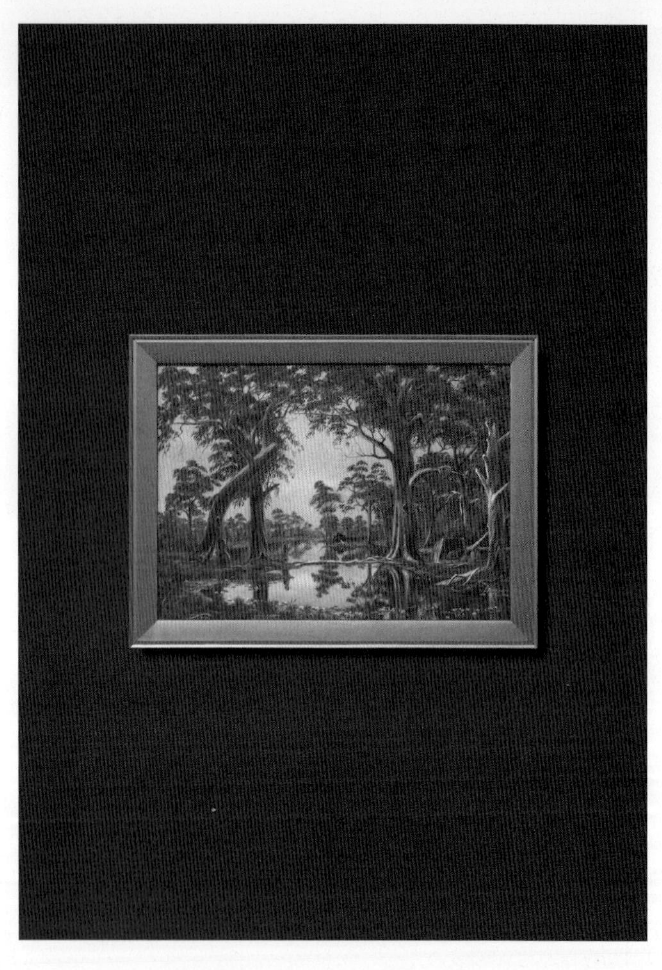

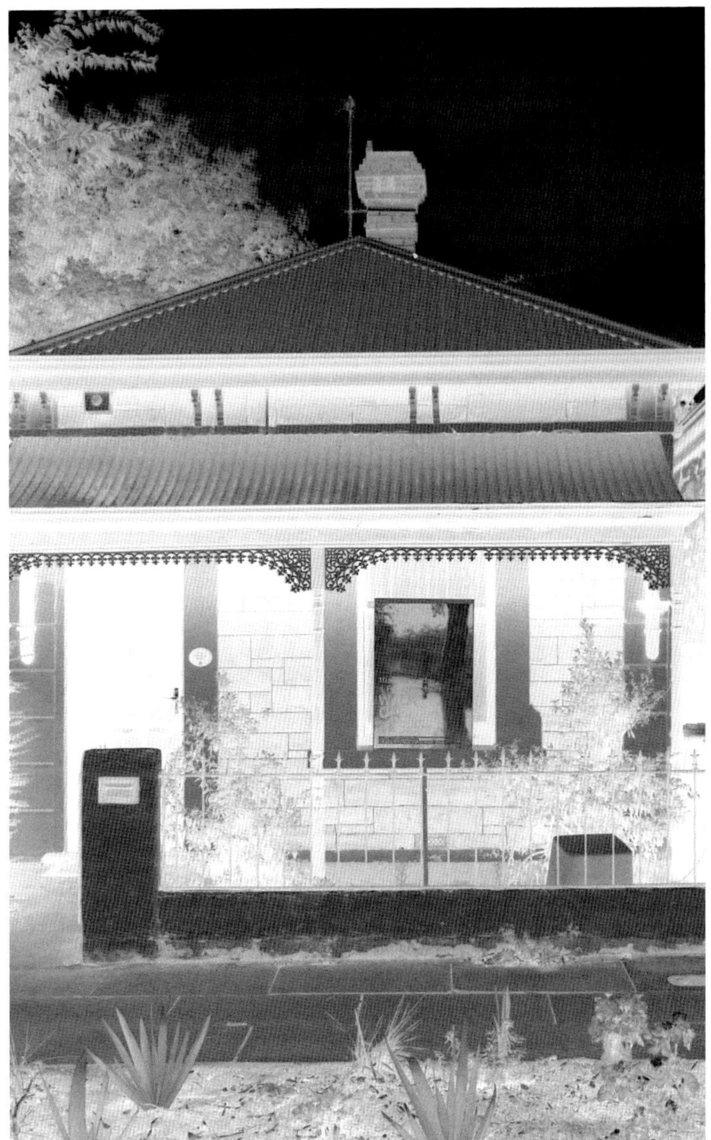

Atkinson's footage shows these Yorta Yorta leaders consistently returning to the sovereign implications of that moment,

a proliferation mirrored in the different versions he paints of the same scene that circulate in various International Exhibitions in Melbourne and around the world in the mid- to late-nineteenth century.

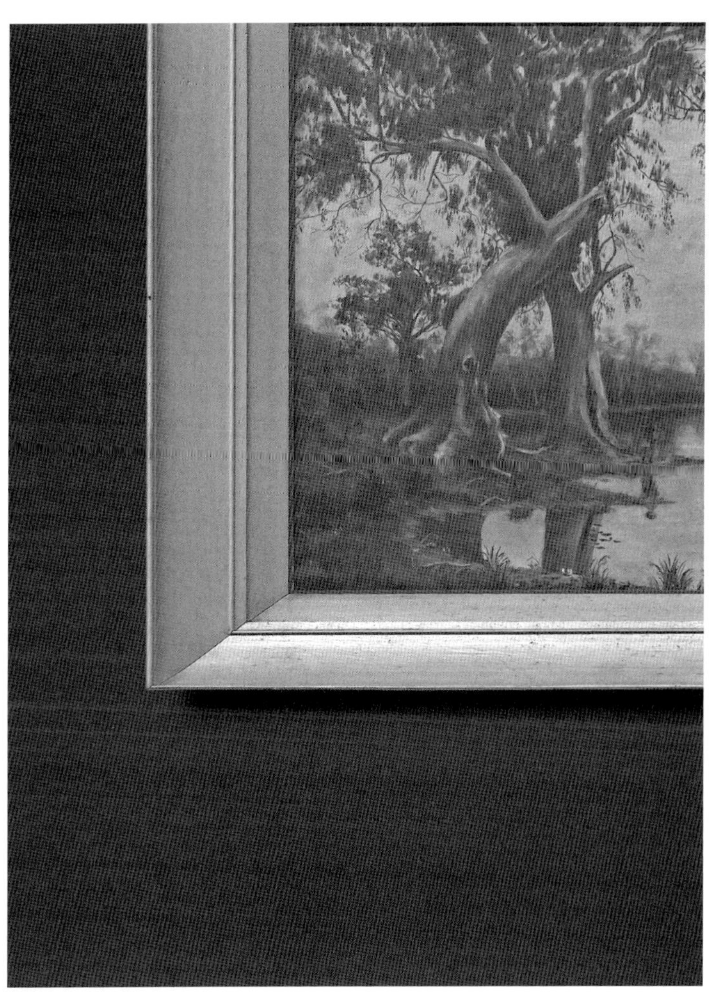

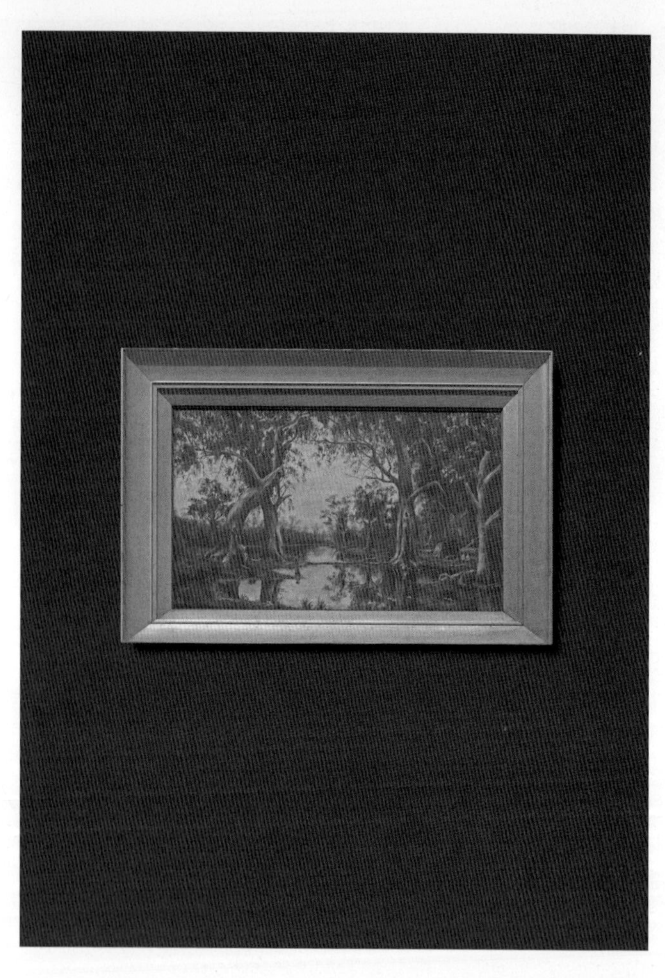

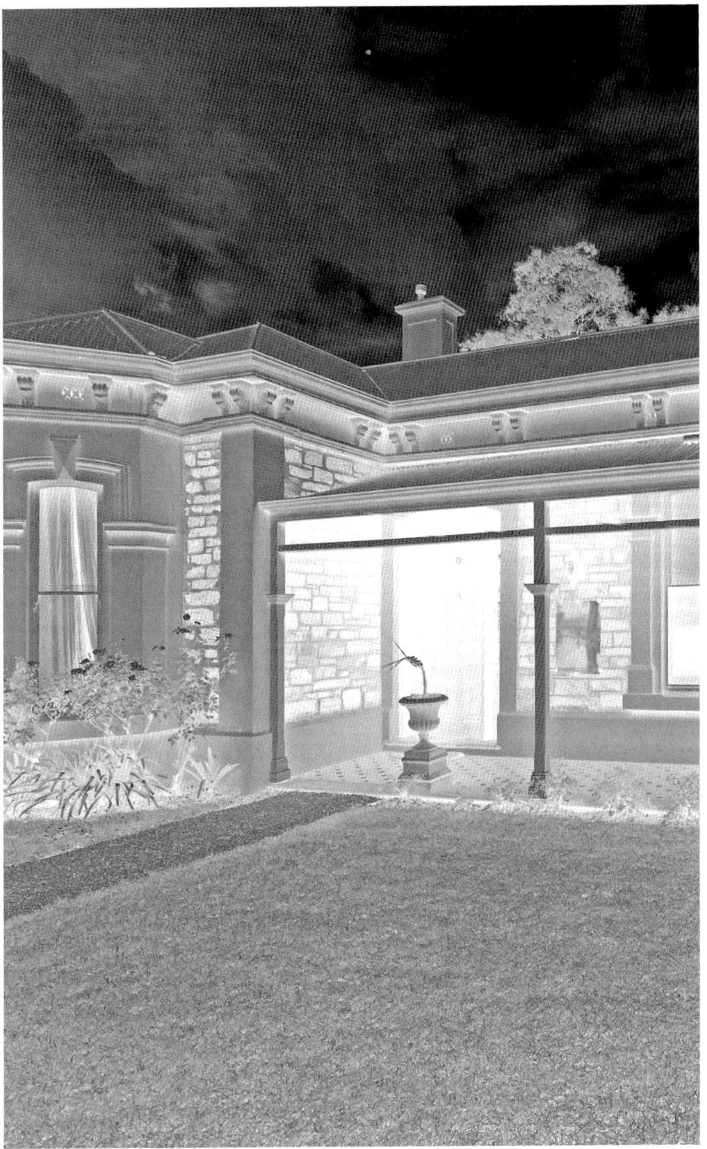

4 February 1939, when Yorta Yorta people cross
the Murray River and protest against the government's
segregation and control policies, asserting their rights
to self-determination, to control of their own affairs.
These implications of 1939

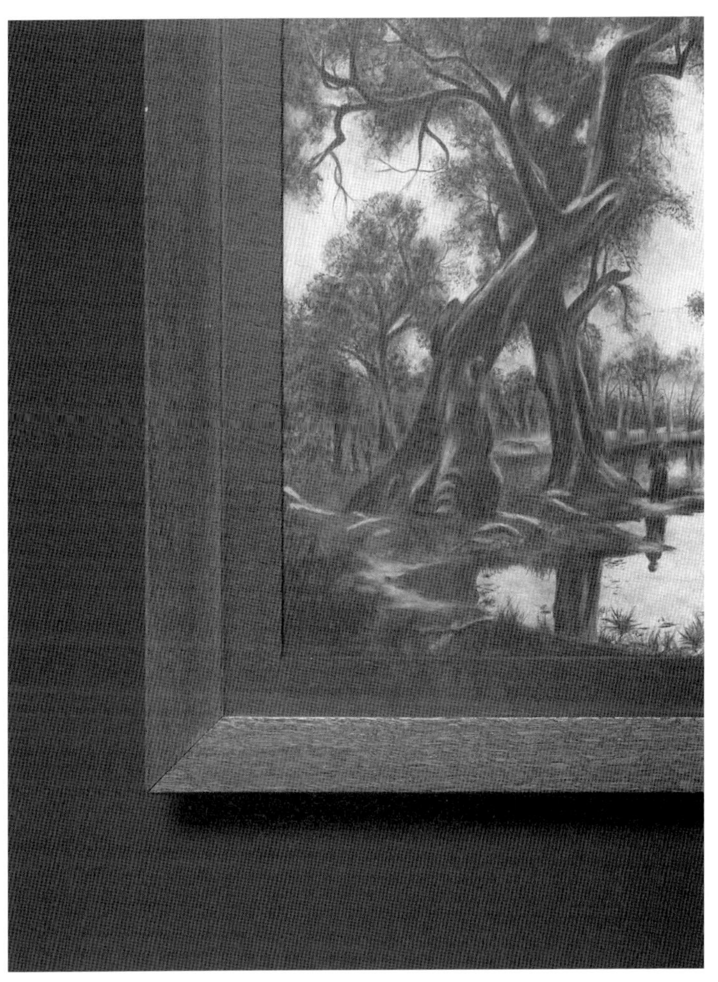

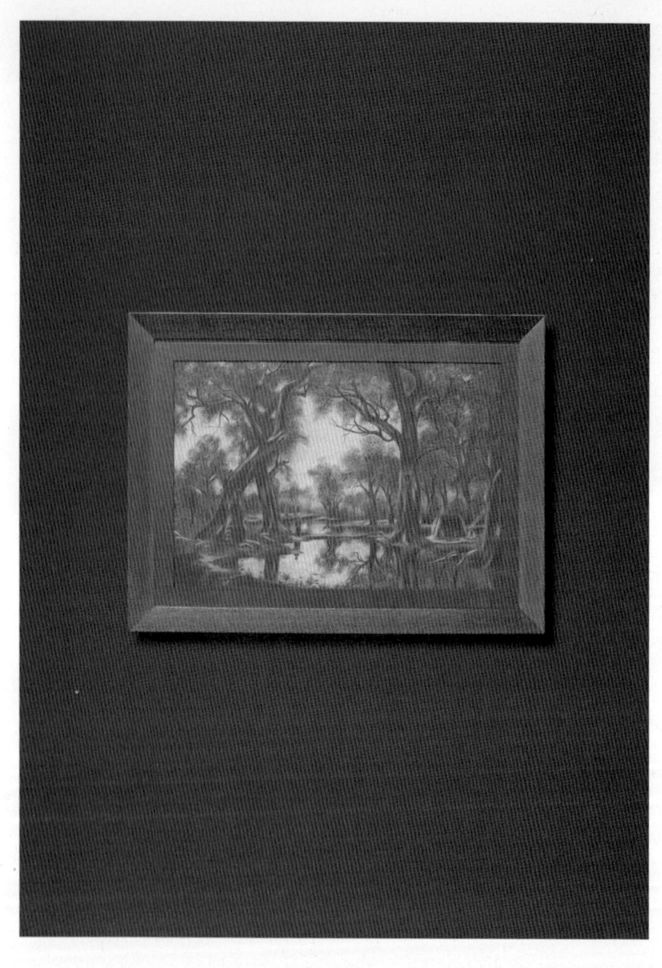

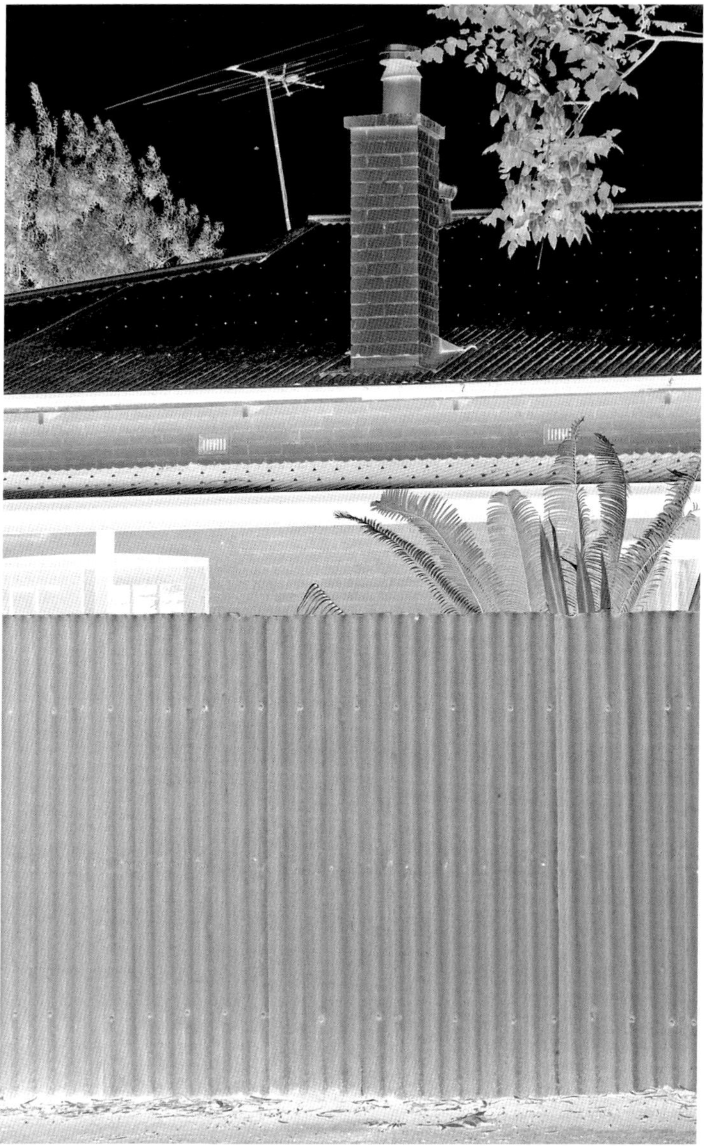

—these rights to self-determination still unrecognised in contemporary Australia—are all the starker in 1988, when Aboriginal people from across Australia gather in protest against bicentenary celebrations in Sydney, reasserting their sovereignty against celebrations of the British invasion, its imposition of alien sovereignty and rule, in 1788.

Widely regarded as the most popular painting in the Art Gallery of South Australia,

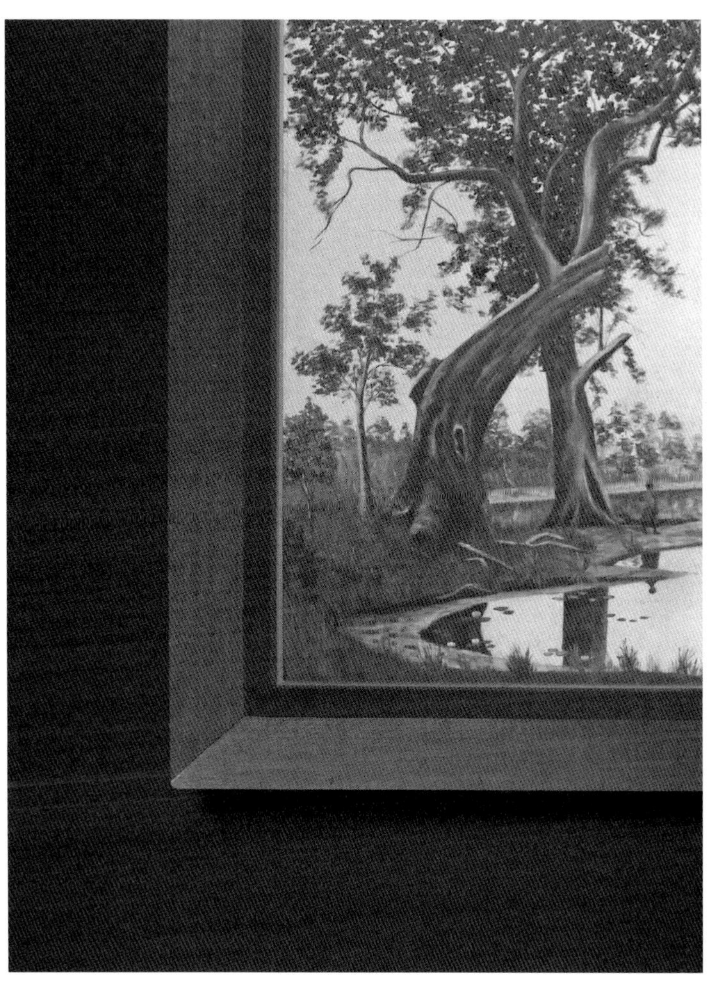

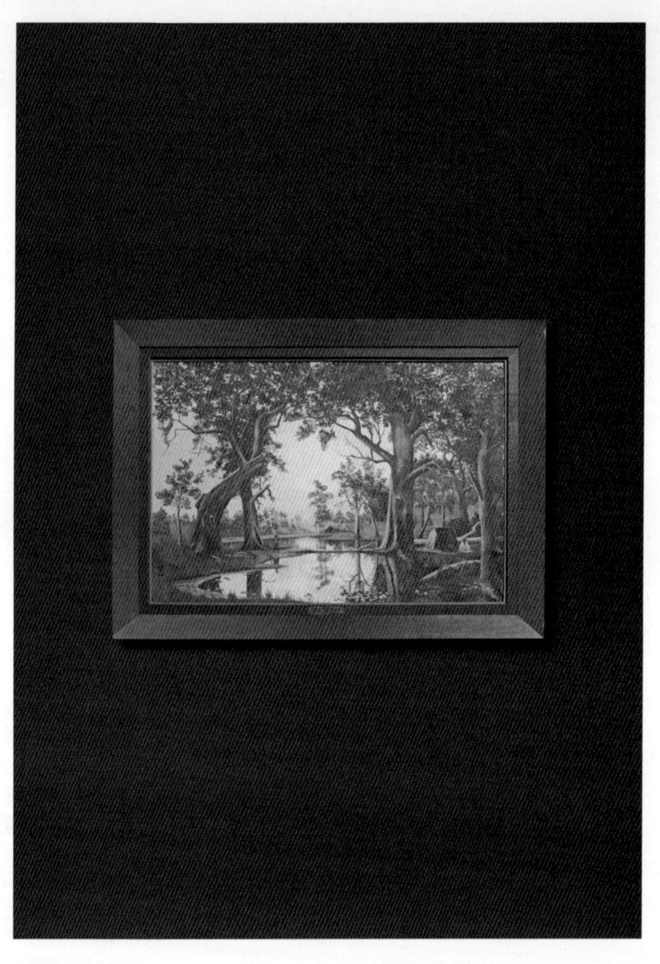

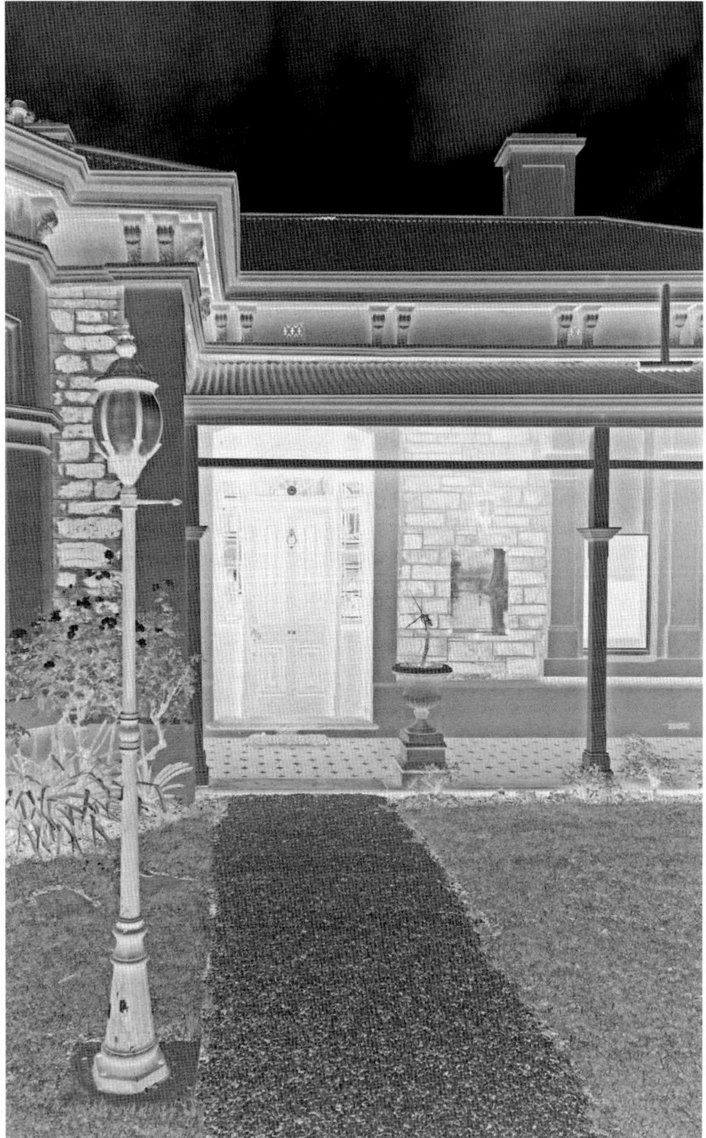

Postscript:

Between 8 October and 2 November 1998, hundreds and hundreds of articles of evidence are presented to the Federal Court in a Native Title claim brought by members of the Yorta Yorta community. These articles of evidence encompass:

where it is the most purchased postcard and poster
from the Gallery shop

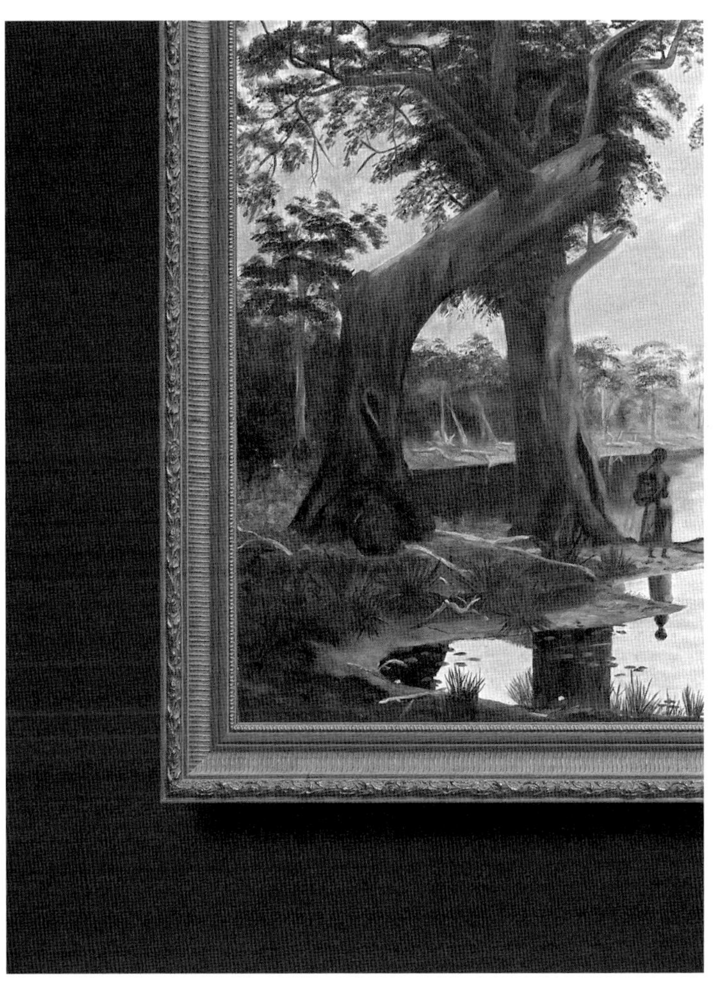

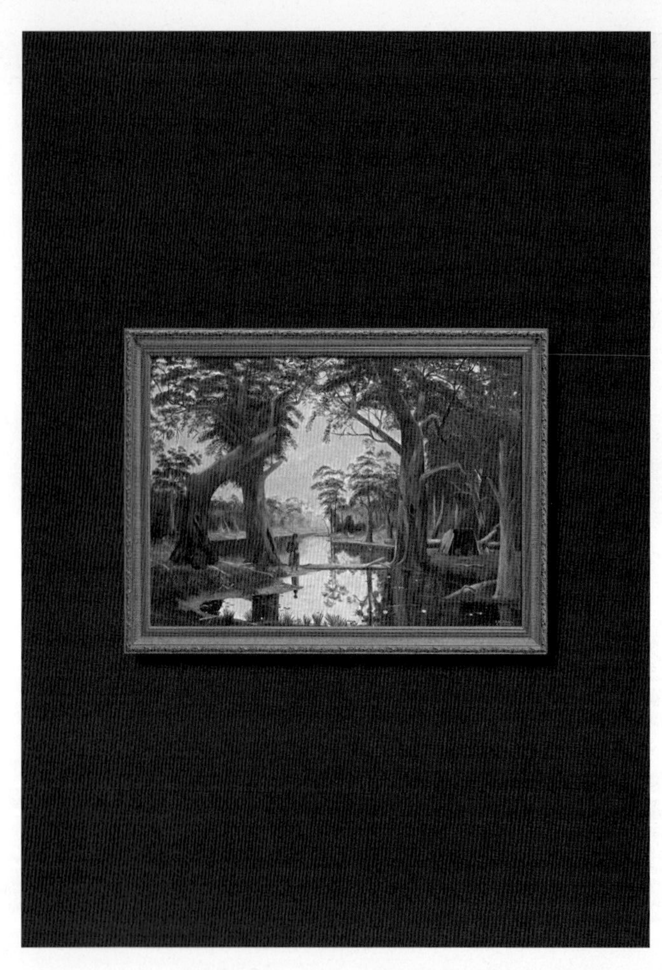

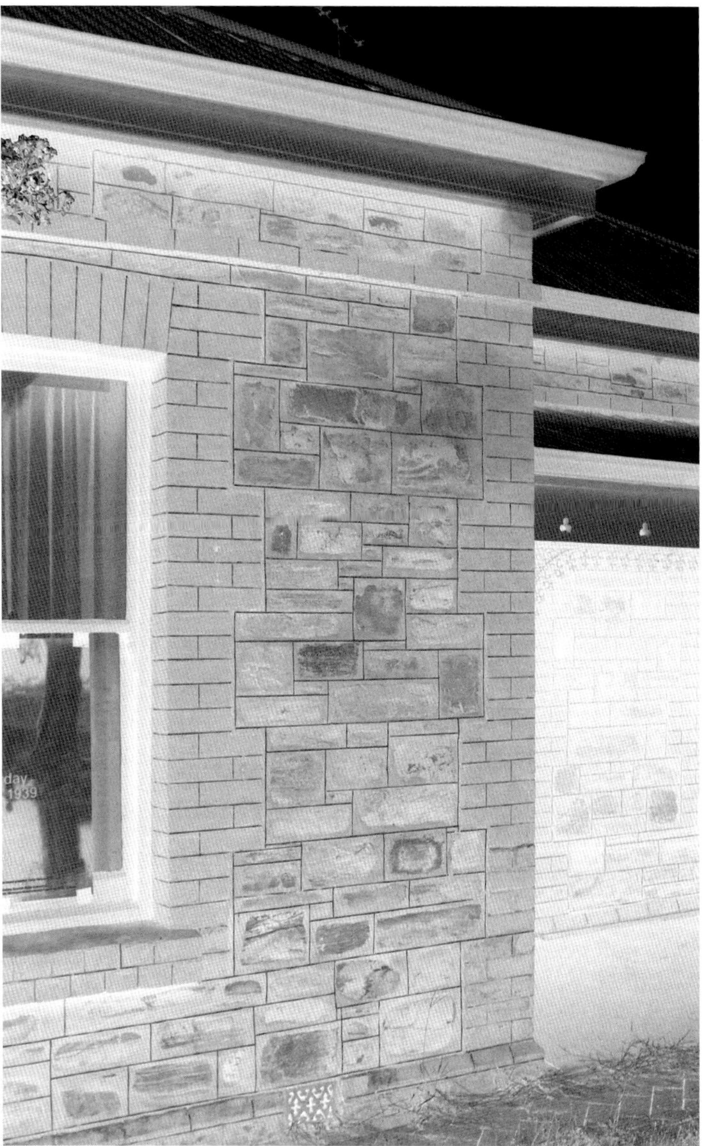

the thousands of years Yorta Yorta people occupied their land before the arrival of Europeans;

and where it also enjoys the distinction of being the Gallery's first acquisition,

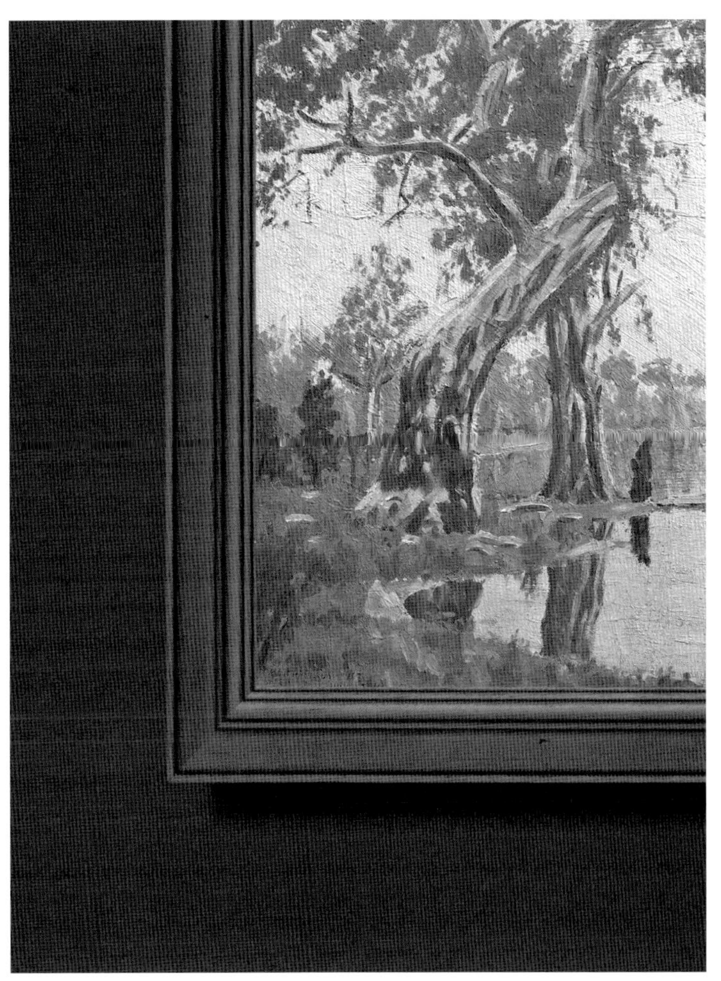

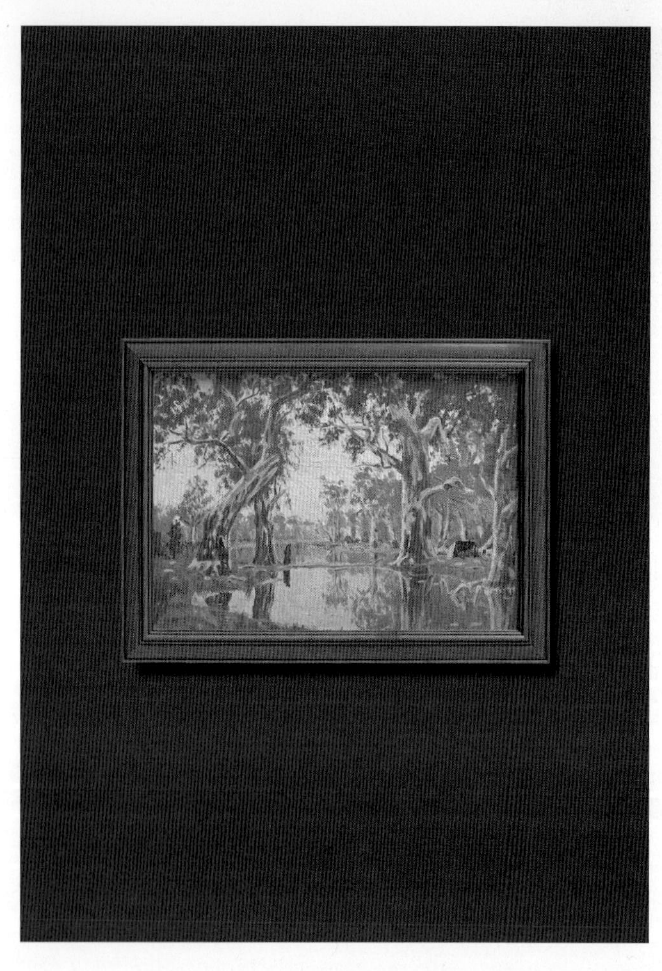

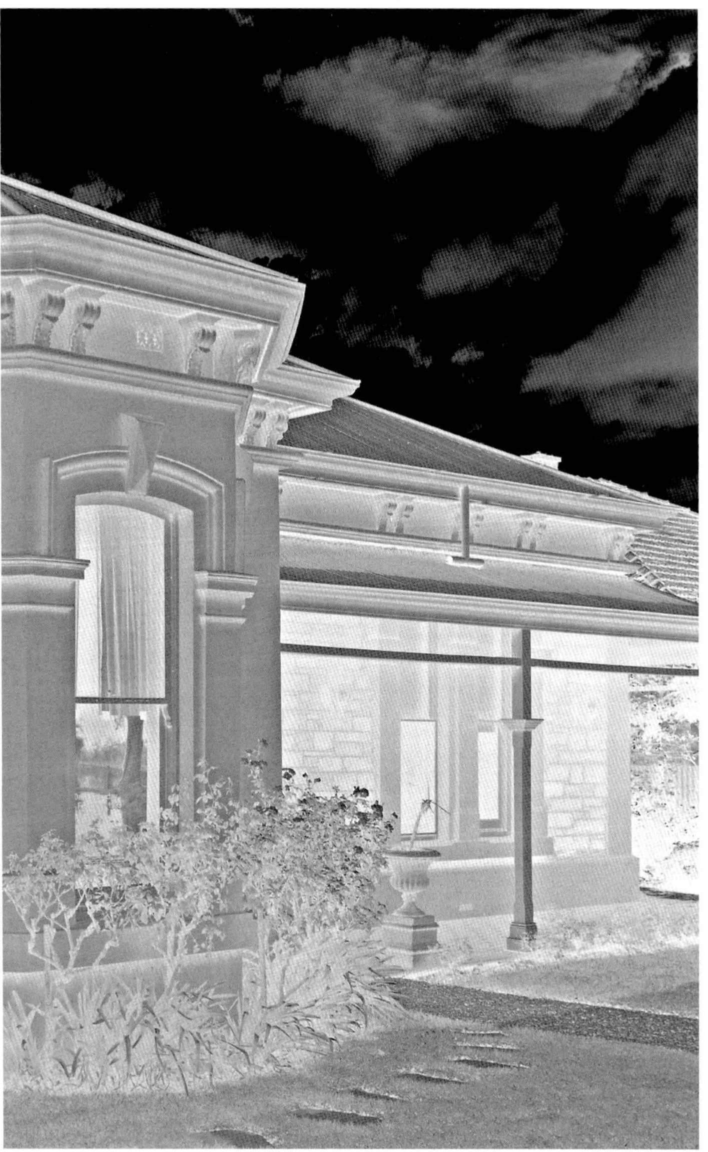

the establishment of a mission for Yorta Yorta people at Maloga on the banks of the Murray River in 1874;

its accession number—0.1—reflecting its position at the collection's origins,

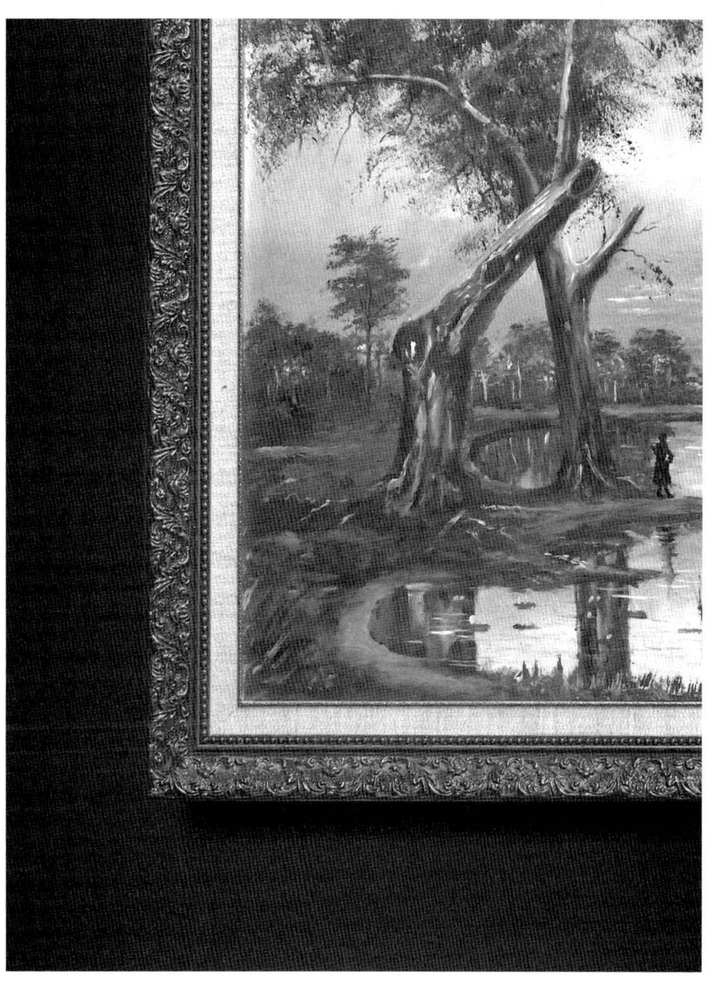

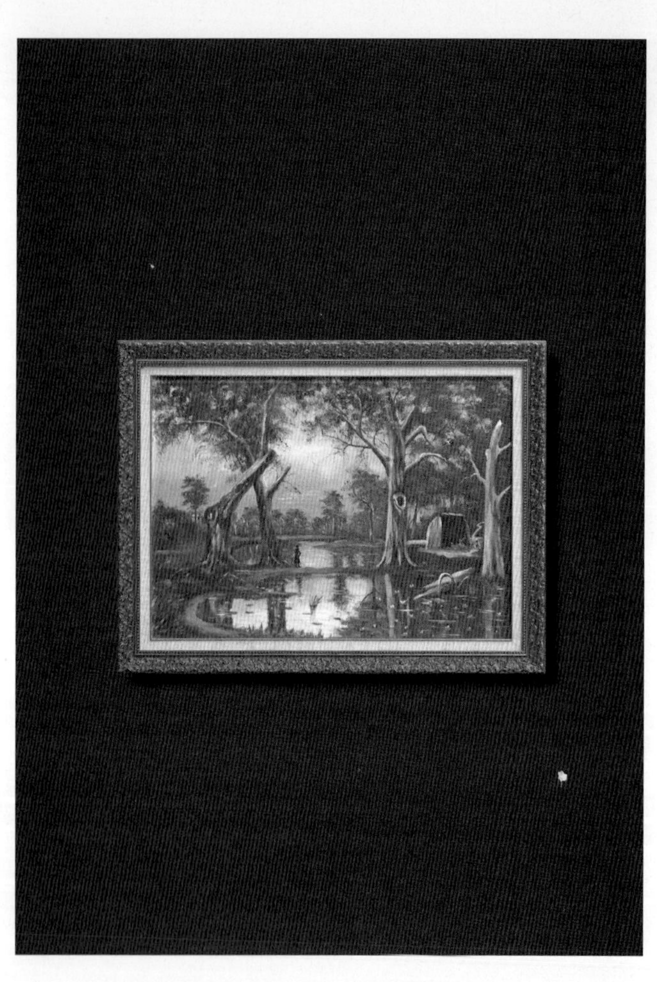

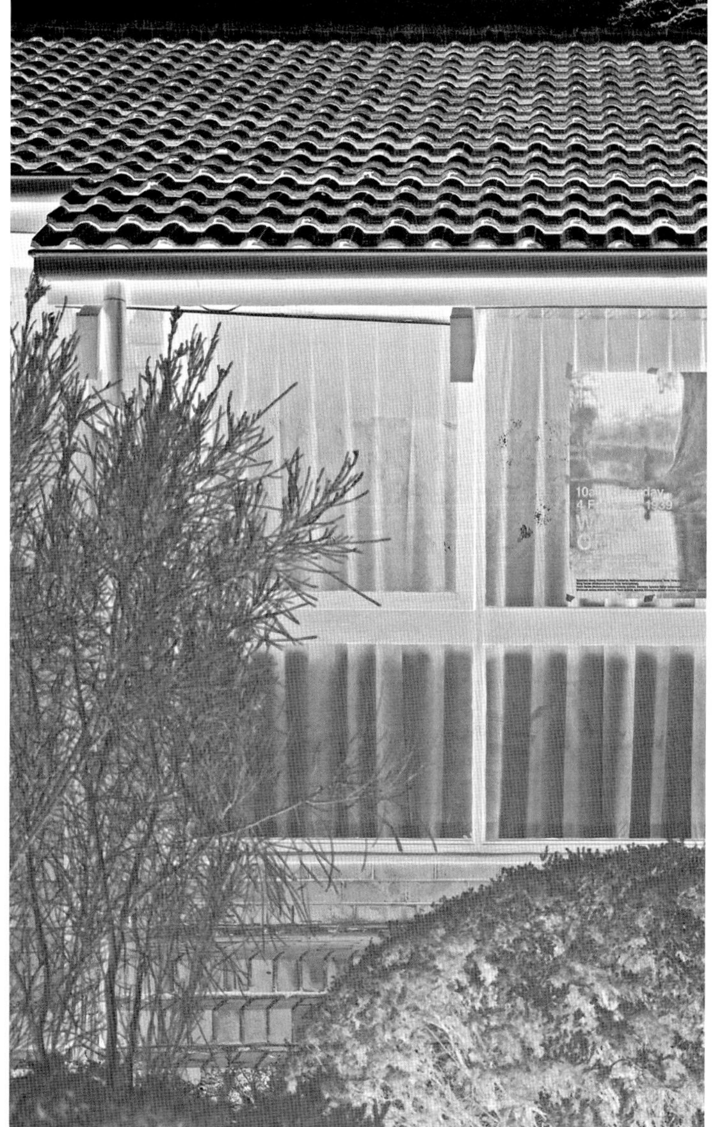

petitioning by Yorta Yorta people for land during the 1880s, and the establishment of Cummeragunja in 1888,

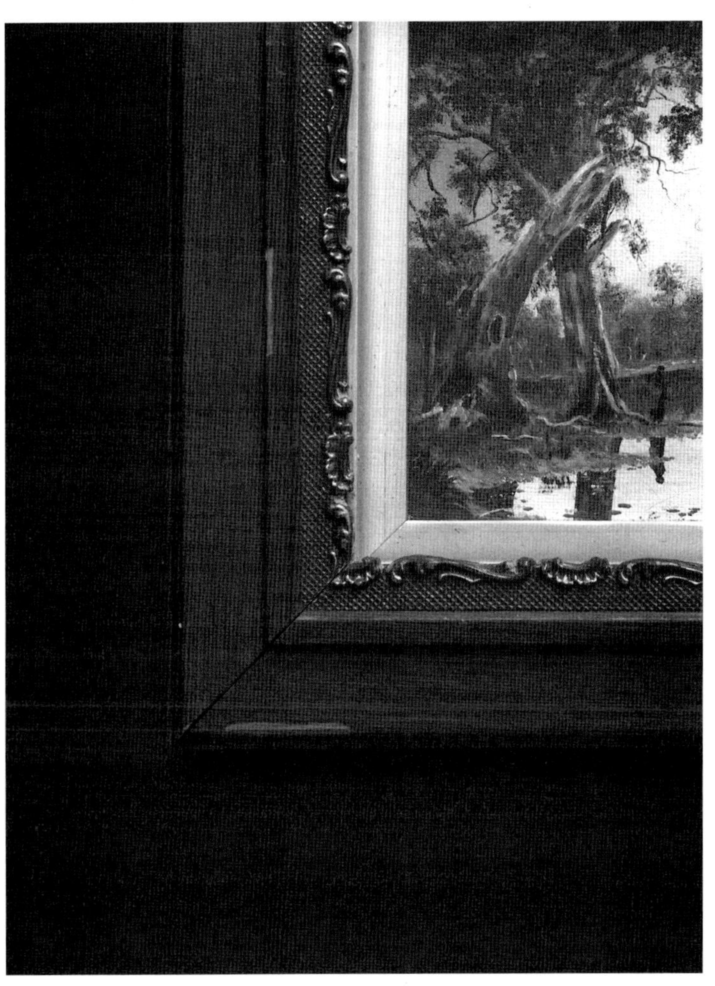

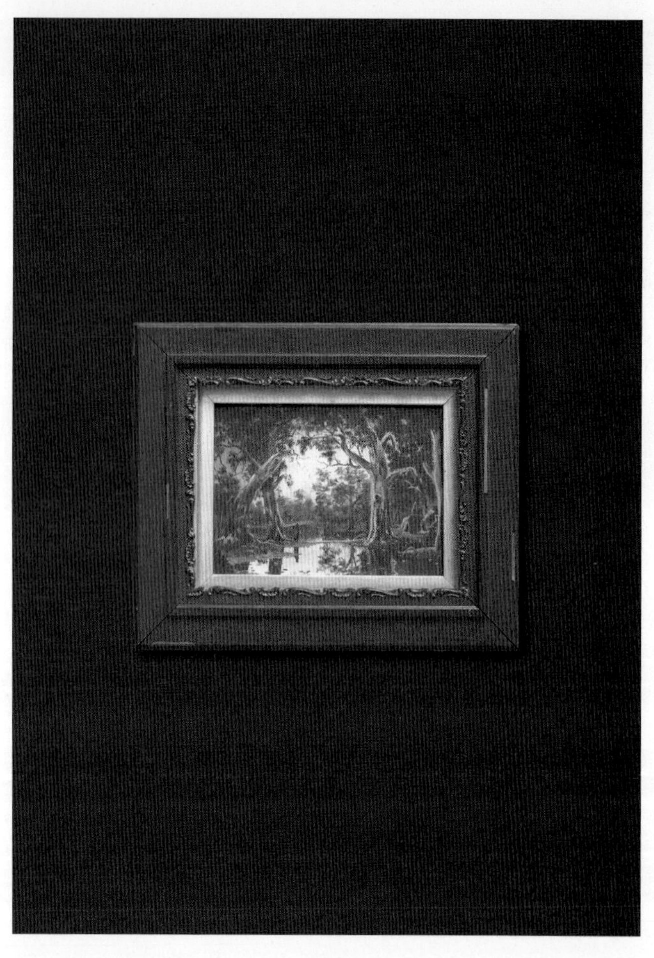

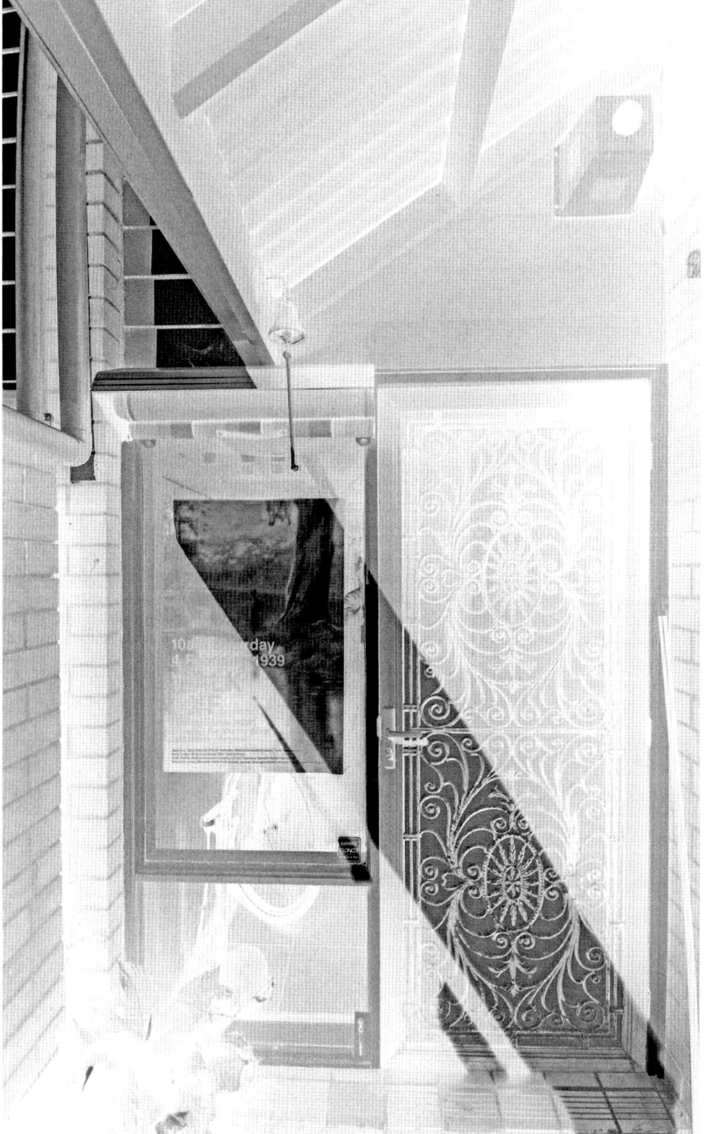

a site on the Murray River chosen by Yorta Yorta elders and named by them “Cummeragunja”, “my home”;

is perhaps most famous through its copies.

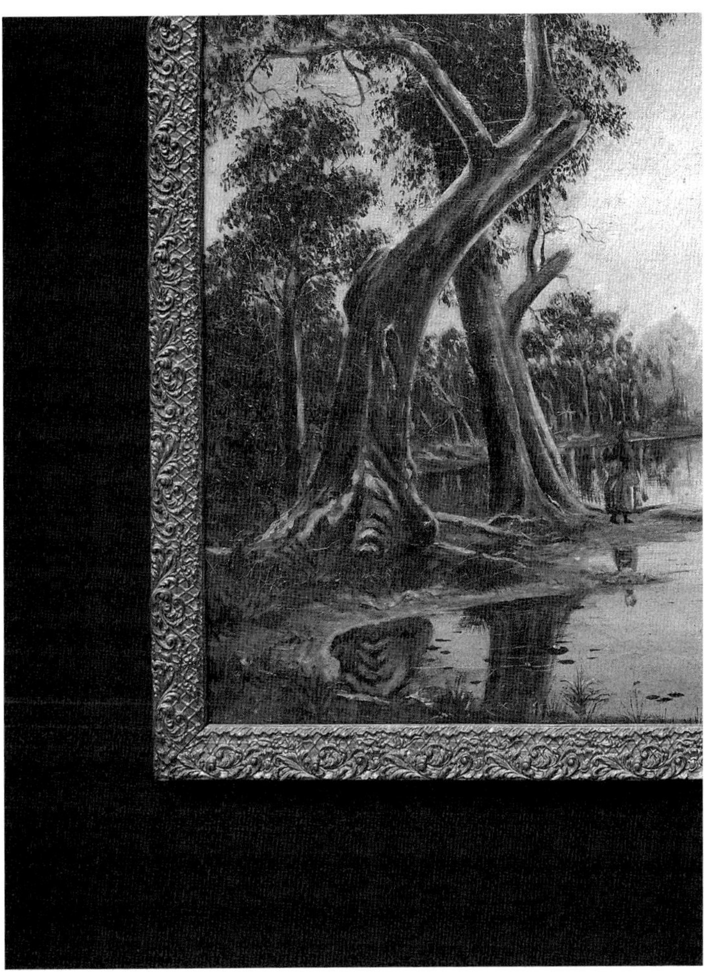

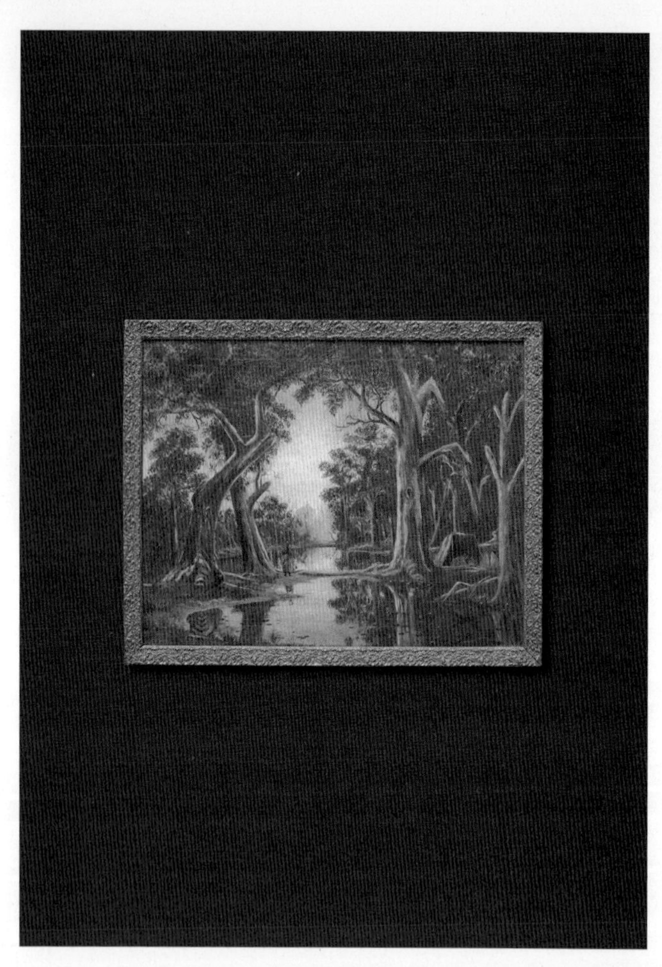

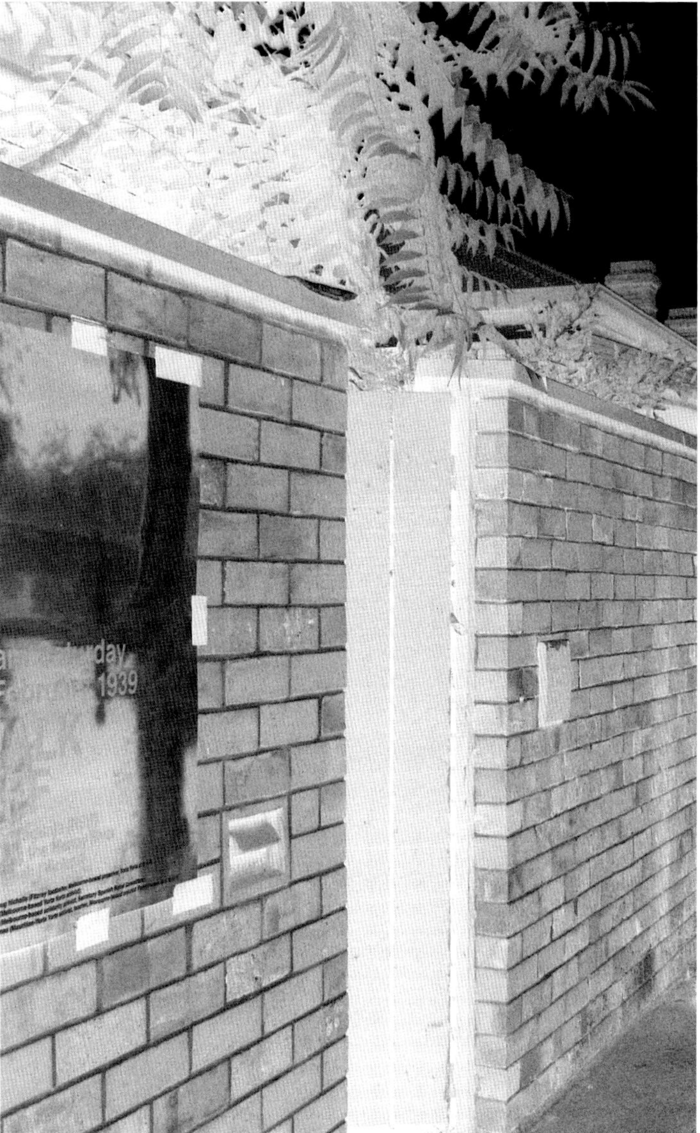

the Cummeragunja Walk Off in February 1939, when 200 of the residents at Cummeragunja cross the Murray River and set up camp on the Victorian bank of the river at Barmah;

The vast number of these copies, painted at different stages in nineteenth- and twentieth-century Australian art history,

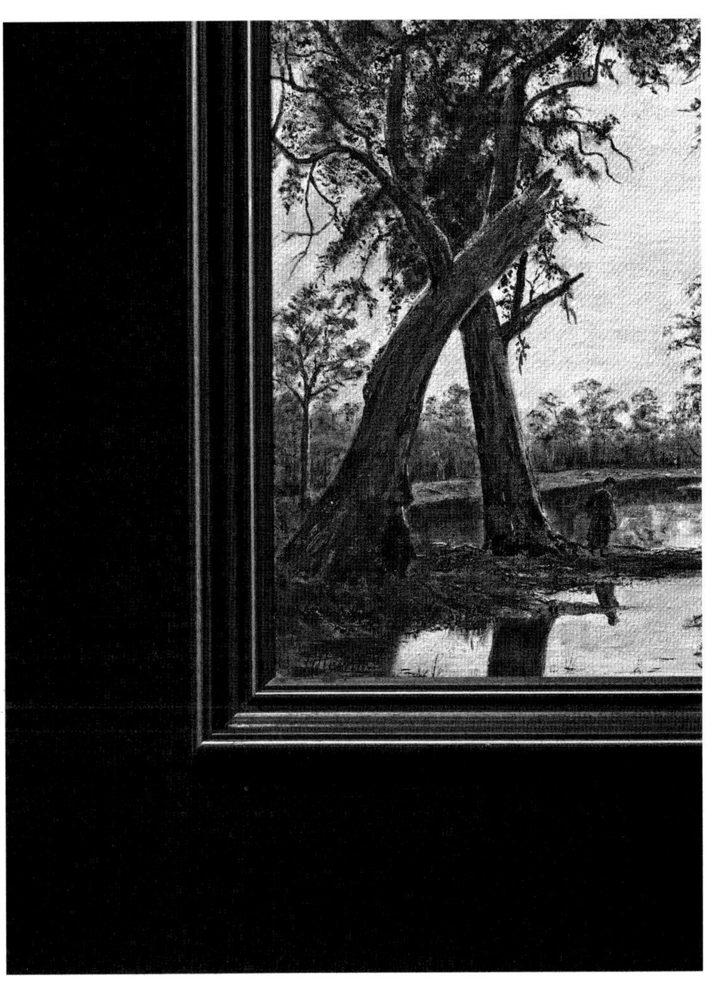

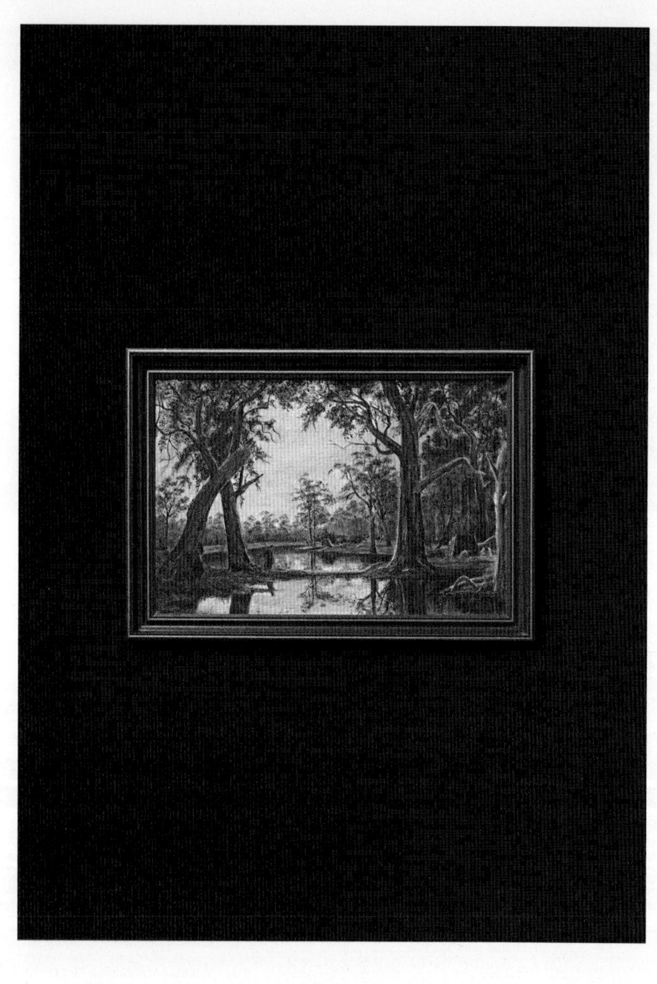

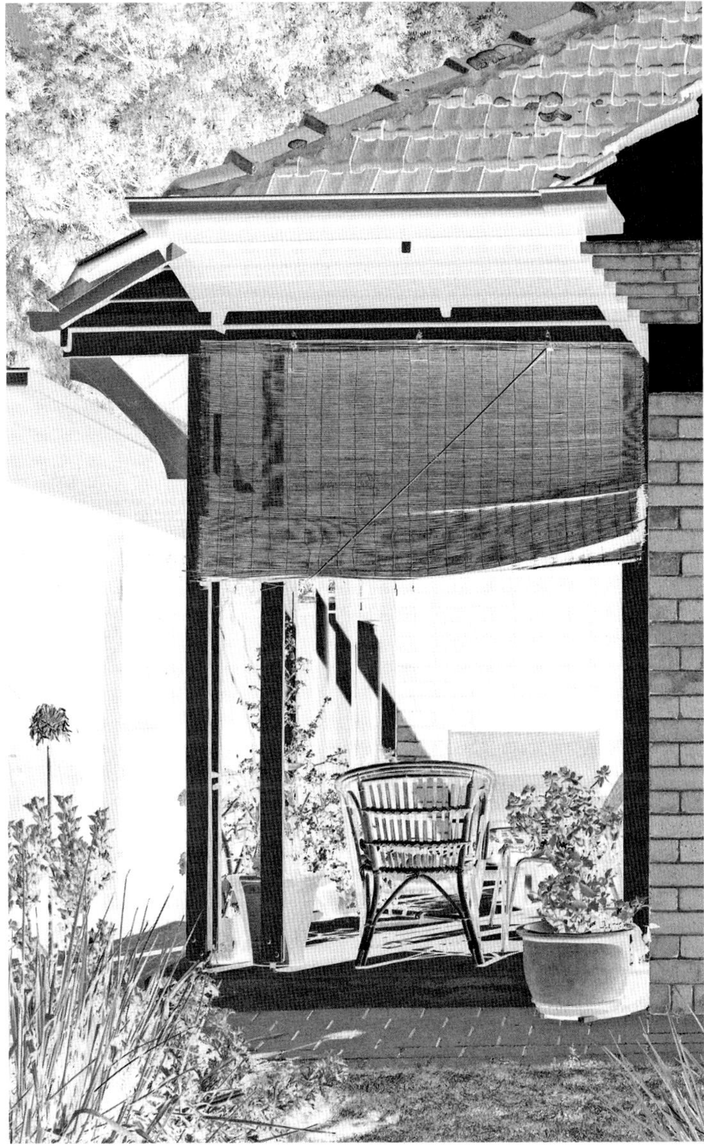

and the continuing agitation for land and rights in the wake of the Walk Off, from Cummeragunja and from the Yorta Yorta diaspora.

from just a few years after the original painting was produced in the 1880s through to the present,

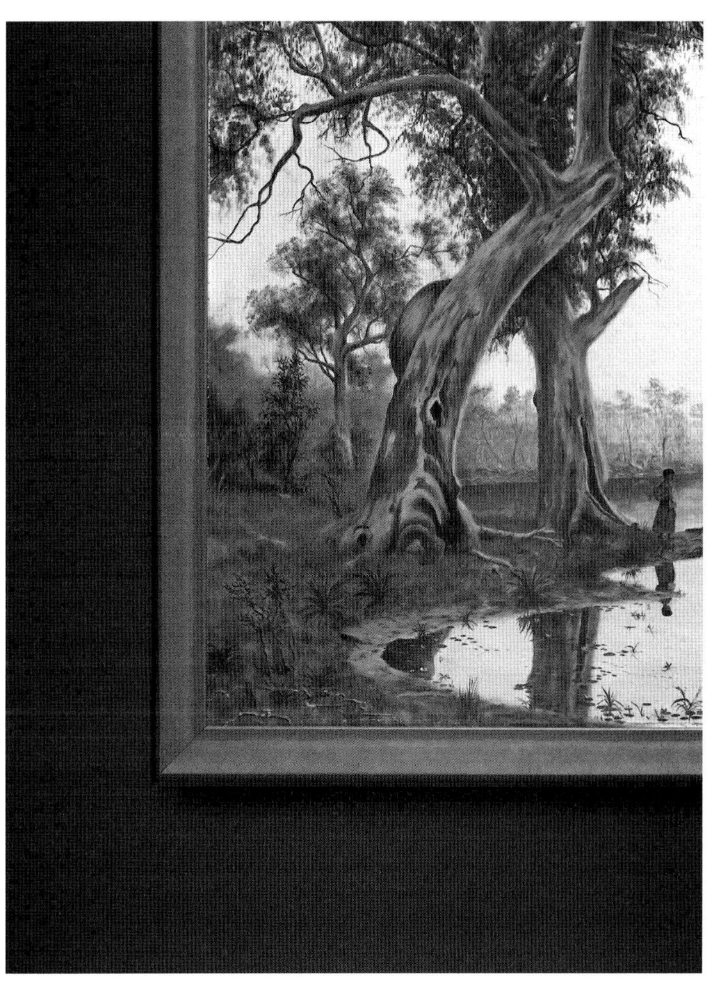

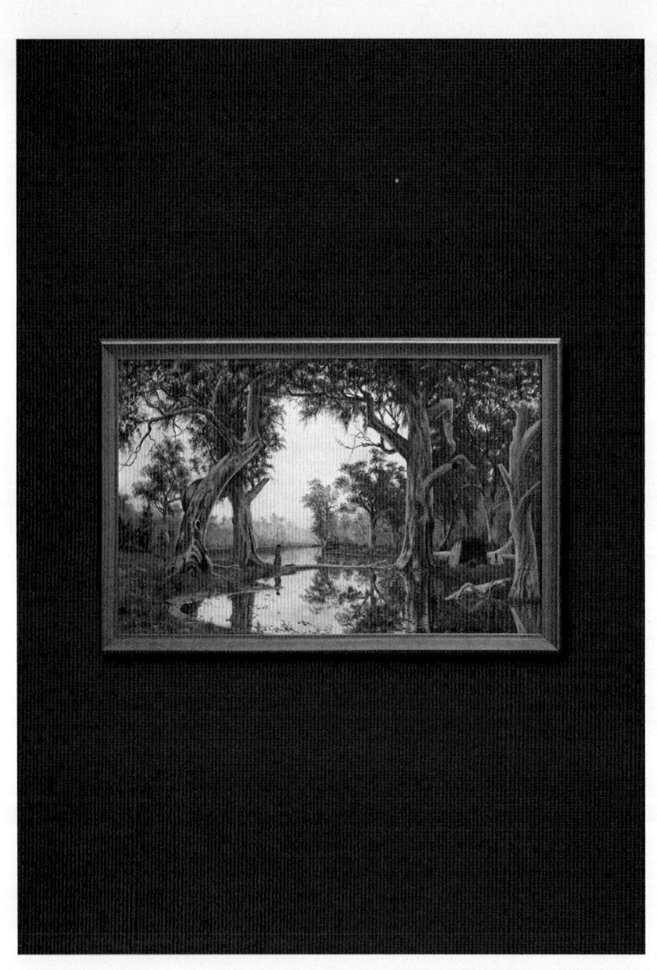

1939

On 18 December 1998, in the face of these articles of evidence, and with a metaphor echoing the tradition of his nineteenth-century forebears—their allegories of gentle and inexorable processes of nature—Justice Olney rules against the Yorta Yorta,

are dotted through homes in and around Adelaide,

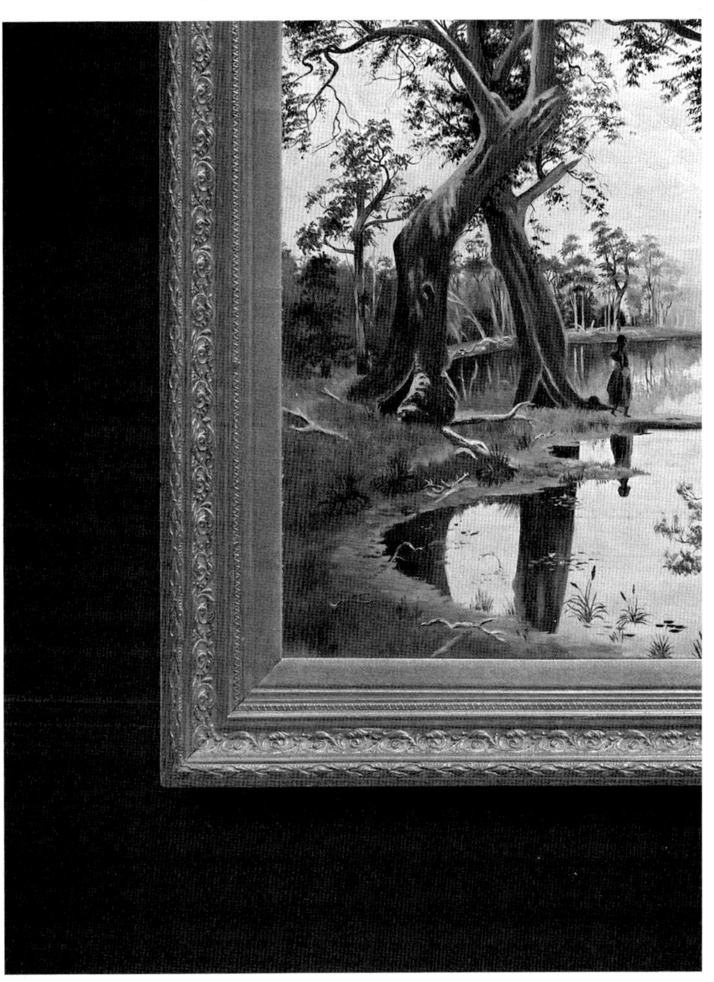

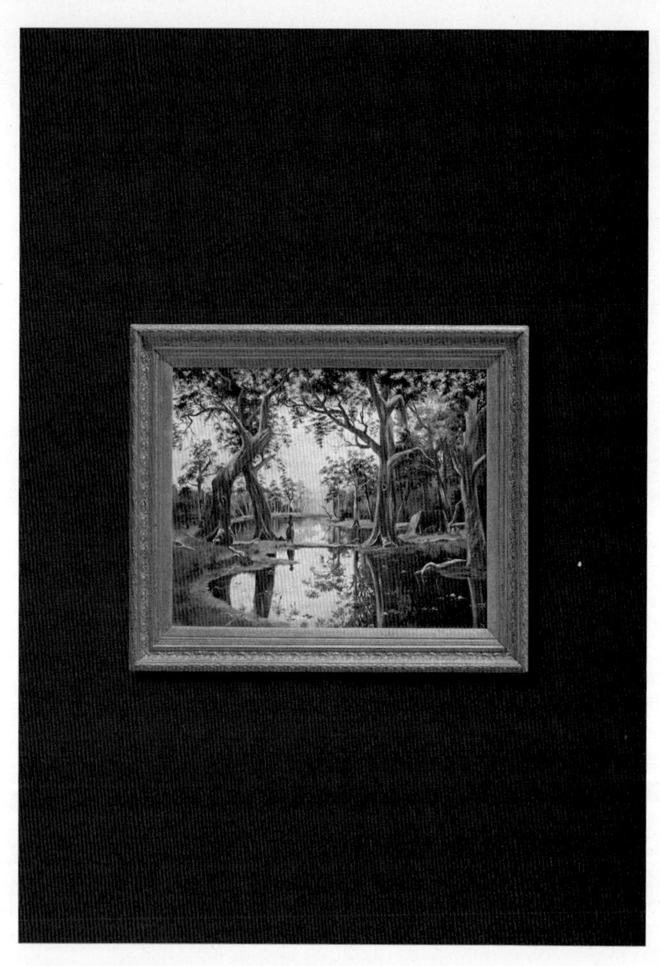

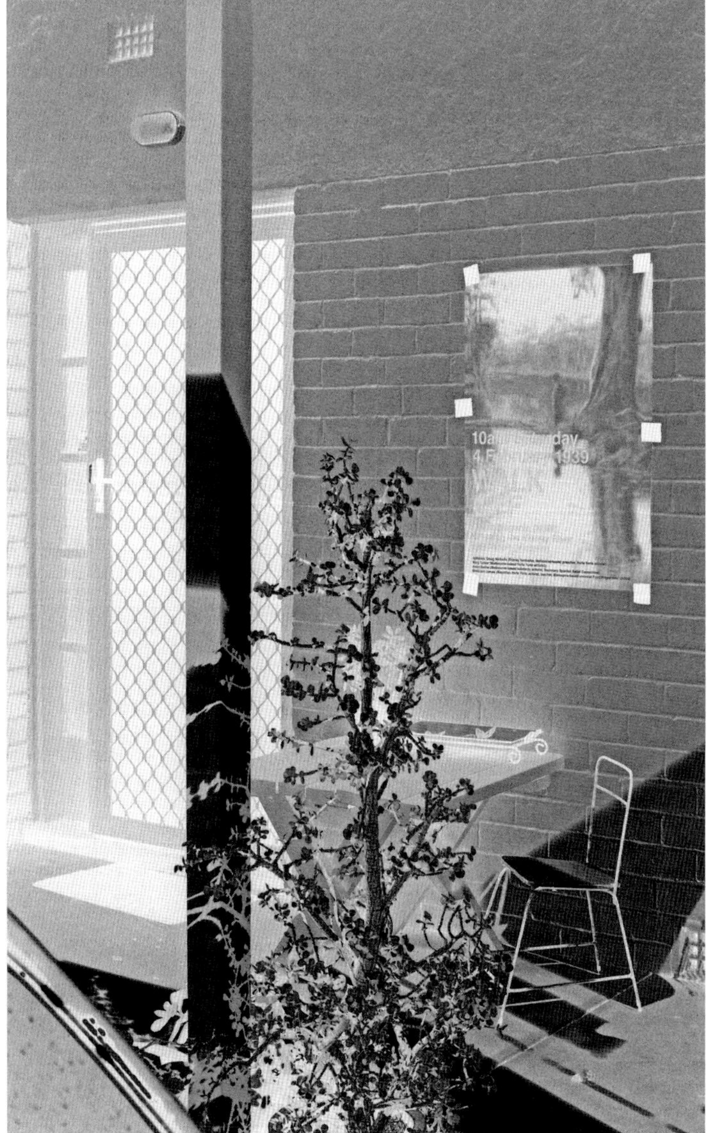

writing that “the tide of history” has washed away their claims.

and reflect its longstanding appeal as the Gallery’s most loved painting.

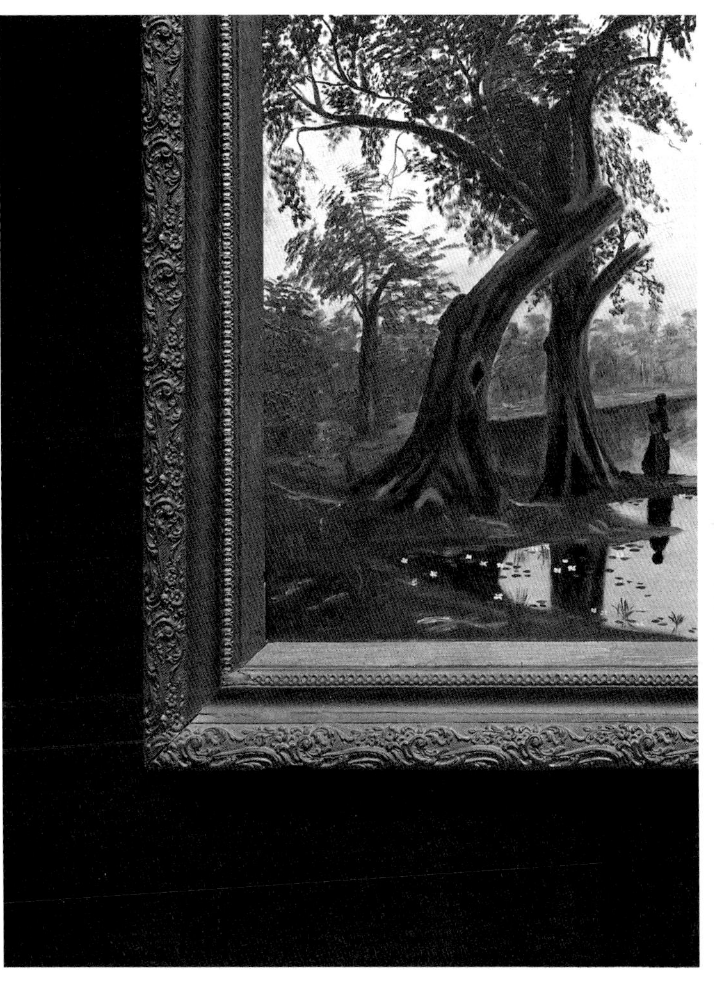

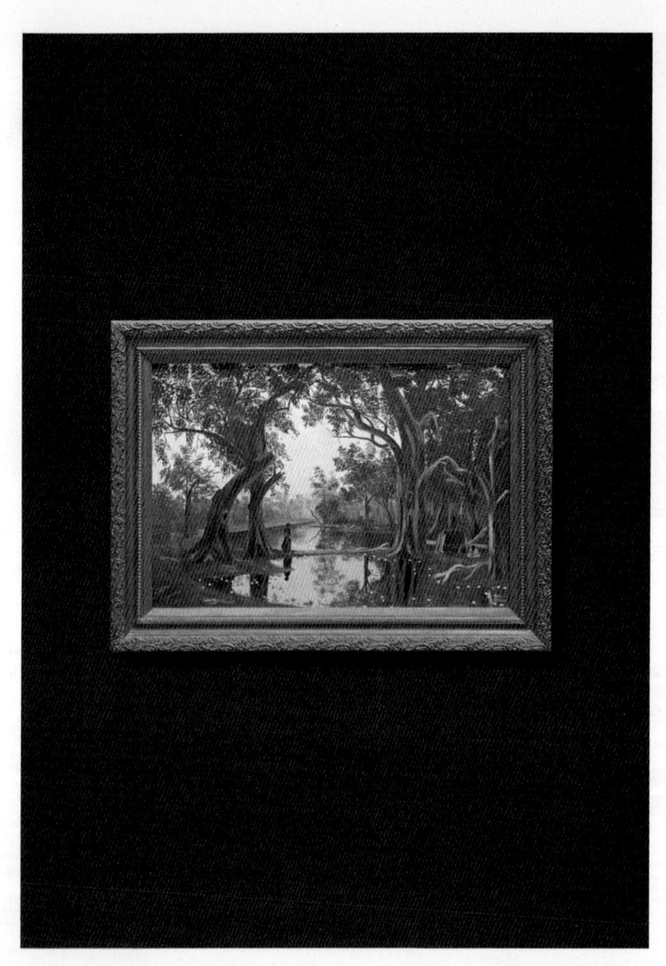